Tales from Michigan Stadium

Jim Brandstatter

SPORTS PUBLISHING L.L.C.

www.SportsPublishingLLC.com

ISBN: 1-59670-015-7

Cover photo by Per H. Kjeldsen.
Back cover and interior photos courtesy of Athletic Media Relations, University of Michigan, unless otherwise indicated.

Publishers: Peter L. Bannon and Joseph J. Bannon Sr.
Senior managing editor: Susan M. Moyer
Acquisitions editor: Mike Pearson
Developmental editors: Mark E. Zulauf and Elisa Bock Laird
Art director: K. Jeffrey Higgerson
Dust jacket design: Joseph Brumleve
Project managers: Greg Hickman and Jim Henehan
Photo editor: Erin Linden-Levy
Vice president of sales and marketing: Kevin King
Media and promotions managers: Jonathan Patterson (regional),
    Randy Fouts (national), Maurey Williamson (print)

Printed in the United States of America

Sports Publishing L.L.C.
804 North Neil Street
Champaign, IL 61820

Phone: 1-877-424-2665
Fax: 217-363-2073
www.SportsPublishingLLC.com

To the men of Michigan
whose effort and commitment to
excellence created the legends that live on
within the confines of Michigan Stadium.

And to Robbie,
whose support and sacrifice have allowed
me to create a career from a hobby.

Contents

vi

Preface

When I was asked about doing the book, I was hesitant. First of all, it would mean a lot of work, and second, it would mean a lot of work!

Anyway, after a couple of months of giving it some thought, I decided it wasn't as daunting a task as I imagined. It would be a challenge, but as they say, nothing ventured, nothing gained. You, the reader, of course, will be the judge of whether anything was gained.

So, as we go forward with *Tales from Michigan Stadium*, I want to tell you that everything in this book isn't exactly from Michigan Stadium. All of it, though, revolves around Michigan football.

It sounds scary to me, but my time around Michigan football spans five decades. I enrolled at the University of Michigan as a freshman in 1968, earned three varsity letters from 1969 through 1971 as an offensive tackle, graduated with a bachelor's degree in 1972, and since then have covered Michigan football as a member of the media.

I have hosted the coach's show *Michigan Replay* since 1980 and have broadcast games either on radio, or tape delayed TV in the 1980s, 1990s, and on into the new millennium.

As a player and broadcaster I have been very fortunate to stay close to the program. It has been a job, but it certainly hasn't been work. During my years in this job, I have experienced a lot and have listened to some wonderful tales that make up the fabric of the Michigan football tradition.

A lot of these stories revolve around the years Bo Schembechler was the coach. Bo remains a good friend, and the guys who played for him have been generous in relating stories to me from this era.

In addition, I have been blessed to have players from days long ago relate their memories of Yost, Crisler, and Oosterbaan among others so I can share them with you.

Some tales from my years as a broadcaster are also included because they have, in some instances, become as memorable as my experiences as a player.

So, from Michigan Stadium, Ferry Field, Ray Fisher Stadium, on the road, and points in between, welcome to *Tales from Michigan Stadium*.

Acknowledgments

A special thanks to all those who were kind enough to share their memories: Larry Adderley, Terry Barr, Frank Beckmann, Jim Betts, Erik Campbell, Don Canham, Lloyd Carr, Anthony Carter, Bob Chappuis, Jim Conley, Tom Coyle, CTC Sports—*The Schembechler Years*, Scott Dreisbach, Don E. Dufek, Don P. Dufek, Stanley Edwards, Bump Elliott, Pete Elliott, Forest Evashevski, Jon Falk, Dave Fisher, Curtis Greer, James Hall, Jerry Hanlon, Pat Hatch, Rich Hewlett, Desmond Howard, Harlan Huckleby, Dick Hunter, Fred Jackson, Doug James, Ron Johnson, Ron Kramer, Rick Leach, Bob Lipson, Don Lund, Rob Lytle, Bruce Madej, Jerry Markbreit, Reggie McKenzie, Jamie Morris, Bobby Morrison, Tom Parkhill, Stan Parrish, Barry Pierson, Cecil Pryor, Hercules Renda, Bo Schembechler, Jim Schneider, Fritz Seyferth, Ron Simpkins, Laverne "Kip" Taylor, Mike Taylor, Dick Vidmer, Derrick Walker, John Wangler, Chuck Winters, Albert Wistert, and Roger Zatkoff.

Tales

"Those Who Stay..."

When Bo Schembechler arrived in Ann Arbor in the winter of 1968 to take over the head-coaching duties at Michigan, he brought with him a belief that to win in the Big Ten, a team had to be tough.

In his first spring as coach, Bo was intent on making Michigan tough. He put his team through one of the most grueling spring practices you can imagine. There was a lot of hitting and a lot of conditioning. None of us had been through this kind of work. It was physically difficult, and the mental pressure was just as intense.

Every day after practice we would drag ourselves into old Yost Field House to the locker room and collapse in front of our lockers. Survival was our goal, and some members of that first team didn't make it. Because of the tough work, there was a great deal of attrition.

Some would show up for practice, and looking ahead to the afternoon, they would just stare at their uniform, not get dressed, and quit the team. Others would come back after a particularly grueling day, slowly take off their uniform, shower, go back to their dorm, and never come back.

One of Bo's motivational techniques was to place signs throughout the locker room. One of our favorites was: "Those who stay will be champions."

One day after yet another rough practice, a group of guys was huddled around this particular sign and chuckling. As I worked my way close enough to see over the shoulder pads, I made out a magic marker scrawl under "Those who stay will be champions." It read, "Those who don't, will be doctors, lawyers, and other important people." At least one of our number who hadn't stayed left the rest of us something to smile about.

1

*Bo Schembechler at his hiring press conference with
Don Canham and outgoing coach Bump Elliott*

As you might guess, Bo immediately removed the magic
marker scrawl and all was back in order.

Ultimately, though, Bo had the last laugh. The next fall,
those who stayed through that difficult first spring were part of
a Michigan team that upset Ohio State 24-12 in one of the great
victories in Michigan football history. We went to the Rose Bowl
as Big Ten champions.

Nuclear Physics

As Michigan prepared for the 1970 Rose Bowl, the NBC
television network came to campus to tape the player introductions.
Back in those days, the starting offensive and defensive units were
taped at their home campus. Each player would stand in front of
the camera and state their name, year in school, hometown, and
major area of study.

Cecil Pryor was a starting defensive end, and he was one of
the toughest guys on our team. He was big, fast, and aggressive.

He played the game with passion, and when you saw him staring out from under his helmet, your knees might shake if you weren't careful. Off the field, Cecil was a very nice guy, pleasant and easy to get along with. He was also a very fun-loving sort.

It was this fun-loving part of Cecil that made the player introductions for the Rose Bowl unique. When it was Cecil's time for his intro, he looked directly into the camera, and with a serious, professorial scowl said, "Cecil Pryor, defensive end, Corpus Christi, Texas, senior, majoring in nuclear physics."

Now Cecil hadn't been anywhere near the physics building in his four years at Michigan. None of us knew about it until we got back to Ann Arbor. We were on the field warming up during the TV pregame.

Today, Cecil is a very successful businessman in the automobile industry. But, back in January 1970, a nation of football fans thought he was on his way to the space program or something like that, thanks to his nuclear physics background!

"Bump" & Pete

In the early 1960s a unique coaching matchup occurred whenever Michigan and Illinois met up on the floor of Michigan Stadium. Chalmers "Bump" Elliott was the head coach at Michigan, and his brother, Pete, was the head coach for the Illini. Both had distinguished themselves as players for the Wolverines in the mid-1940s but as coaches, they were enemies.

According to both men, there wasn't a lot of banter as they met each other prior to their head-to-head matchups, but there was one year that clearly stands out.

In 1960, Michigan trailed the Illini 7-0 in the first half. Michigan had just crossed over the 50-yard line and into Illinois territory, but were facing a fourth-down-and-long. Bump remembers as if it were yesterday, "I crossed him up and went for it..."

Pete growls, "It was a terrible strategic call."

Bump smiles, "... And we made it."

"It was still a terrible call," Pete grumbles.

"We went on to score," remembers Bump, "and after we scored, we went for two and made it to take an 8-7 lead. It held up, too."

"It was still a terrible call," Pete mumbles.

"So what about that time I called a pass down by the goal line and your guy intercepted and returned it for a touchdown?" says Bump.

"That was a great call," says Pete, smiling.

The battling Elliott brothers: Pete of Illinois and Bump of Michigan.

"Sally" What?

In the spring of 1969, the players were learning an entirely new offense and defense. Bo Schembechler had been hired from Miami of Ohio as head coach, and we were undergoing a bit of culture shock.

As we gathered under the stands of the baseball stadium, Bo was going over the offensive playbook. The numbering system was different, the formations were different, and the terminology was new. At one point Bo said, "OK, now we get to our reverse. We call it a 'Sally.'"

He had his back to us and was diagramming on a blackboard. We were between the ages of 18 and 21, and some of us looked at each other quizzically, like, what does he mean, "Sally?" We were a bit confused, and apparently when Bo turned around after finishing his diagram, he sensed he'd lost us.

"What?" he asked.

We kind of murmured as a group.

"What, you mean you guys don't know about Sally Rand?"

We had no clue.

At that point, Bo launched into an explanation of Sally Rand. She was a stripper during the burlesque era. She was beautiful, and she had a gimmick that was better than any other stripper's. She used these feathered fans to cover her up. You knew she was naked underneath, but she would tease you with a momentary glimpse before the feathers covered her.

"That's why we call this play a 'Sally'; it's our naked reverse," Bo said triumphantly.

We all groaned. Bo had this playful grin on his face, but the fact was, we did call it a "Sally." I think the team still does.

There were times in tight games, when I was standing next to him on the sidelines ready to run in with a play, when I would hear Bo say over the phone to assistant coach Jerry Hanlon in the press box, "You want to run the 'Sally'?"

We made big plays with the "Sally" all the time. After games I would be partying with friends talking about the game. They'd ask about the play, and I'd say we caught the opponent off guard with our "Sally." Then I'd have to explain the whole story. Now you know, too.

No Ordinary Man

When Schembechler arrived in Ann Arbor, he made it clear to all of us that we would be a physical football team. With that in mind, our practices were not for the faint of heart. We got after it in practice, and it translated to games.

During one of these physical practices, a scrimmage took place. Bo was working the sidelines, calling the plays and sending them in to the offense. The defensive coaches were operating from the sidelines too, working the substitution patterns and getting us game-ready. On one play, Bo was looking down at his notes to call the next play, and the play being run on the field broke down. Instead of going away from him, it came right at him. He was unaware until the last minute, and three or four guys plowed into him at full speed.

Bo was upended, his hat flew one way, the papers another, and his body yet another. Linebacker Mike Taylor, one of the hardest hitters at Michigan, was in the middle of the play. Mike remembers that it got very quiet. As he got up from the pile, he saw Bo trying to get his bearings. The trainers and assistant coaches all came over to see whether Bo was alright. After a few moments, Bo struggled to his feet. Taylor remembers Bo saying gruffly, "Where's my hat?"

Somebody gave it to him, and he put it back on. He then wobbled back to his spot on the sideline. Nobody had moved during the time he had been down, and there was a crowd of players and coaches around him. Bo looked up at everyone, slowly turning around to see the circle of concern. He then looked back down at his play sheet, and without looking up, speaking to nobody, but loudly enough so everyone could hear, Bo said, "Hell, that would have killed any ordinary human!"

Mike Taylor remembers jogging back to his position on the field laughing out loud.

Mike Taylor (No. 33) in a more menacing situation.

Getting Hurt

It was important for all of us to play tough. It was important for Bo to know that we were tough, and he had an interesting way of letting us know.

If you ask him, Bo will tell you that his favorite spot on a coaching staff, besides the head-coaching position, would be the offensive line coach. He had a special place in his coaching heart for the offensive line. As an offensive lineman, you found that out before too long, and Bo let you know you had better be a special guy if you were going to play for him on the offensive line.

On occasion during practice, an offensive lineman would get kicked hard in the shin, or a 260-pound guy would step on your hand, or another 260-pound guy would roll up on your ankle or knee. These occurrences were never pleasant, and there were times when you stayed down on the ground for a moment or two to let the pain subside before heading back to the huddle.

As you were lying there, Bo would trot over to you or yell out at you. His eyes stared into the hurt, and he'd say, "C'mon, get up, don't you know? Offensive linemen aren't allowed to get hurt."

Then, as you got up and limped back to work, Bo would turn and bark, "You're not allowed to limp, either!"

For the most part, we never limped after Bo let us know the rules for the offensive line.

The Movie M*A*S*H

This story actually happened, and I'm not changing the names to protect the guilty.

It was the fall of 1970. The movie *M*A*S*H* had just been released, and one night a few of the guys went to see it. One of those guys was a very good friend of mine named Tom Huiskens, a tight end from Bay City, Michigan. We all called him "Husky Pup." We all enjoyed the movie. After it was over, we went back to our dorms, and that was the end of it, I thought.

That Saturday we played Minnesota at Michigan Stadium. We were in the process of blowing the Gophers away to retain the Little Brown Jug. "Husky" and I were backing up the starters at strong tackle and tight end at the time, so we didn't see much action until it was mop-up time.

With a couple minutes to go in the game, we got the call. We ran a couple of plays, and with the clock running out we had about one more play to run. We ran up to the line of scrimmage, and as we were getting down in our stances, I heard Husky say, "Hey buddy, this time this guy is going to knock your [blankin'] head off."

I jerked my head around and saw "Husky" talking to the guy from Minnesota directly across from me! It was a line right out of the movie.

As we settled into our stances, both of us started to laugh, and when the ball was snapped, neither of us moved. The guy from Minnesota drilled me before I even moved. Luckily the play went away from us, so the damage wasn't serious.

The problem came the next day while reviewing the game films with Bo. He looked at every play in the game, and when we got to that one, "Husky" and I sank down in our chairs.

"What the hell is going on with you, Brandstatter? How the hell can I play with a guy that doesn't remember a snap count?" bellowed Schembechler.

"Husky Pup" escaped the wrath of Bo. I had to take it, thanks to the movie *M*A*S*H*.

Bloomington, Right?

Before I started broadcasting Michigan football on the radio, I had the opportunity to broadcast the games on television tape-delay. In the mid-1970s the outlet I was working for was the old ON-TV network.

We broadcast all the games, both home and away. When we traveled, the play-by-play man, Larry Adderley, and I would meet the game producer, Rockey Flinterman, and our director, and our pilot at the airport on Saturday mornings. We'd fly a twin engine private plane to the city where Michigan was to play.

One weekend we were on our way to Bloomington, Indiana, for an afternoon game against the Hoosiers. All was well until we got a few miles out from the Bloomington airport. We were running a tight schedule for the 1 p.m. start, so Rockey got on the plane's radio and called the car rental desk to make sure our car was ready when we landed to speed things along.

The call came back to us that the car rental company had no record of our reservation. Well, this got Rockey steamed. He had made the reservations himself earlier in the week. Rockey called back to the girl on the desk and gave her the confirmation number, the credit card number, his frequent renter number, and made it clear to her that he was very unhappy that they had screwed up his reservation.

When we landed and got to the rental desk, Rockey continued this full-court press on the poor clerk at the desk. She was very apologetic and explained she had no idea how the reservation had been lost. We were standing around trying to stay out of it, because Rockey was still mad, and he was making sure this clerk knew it.

Finally, we got the keys to the car, and we headed for the door to get to the game. On our way out, Rockey turned to the girl and growled, "Can you give us directions to the stadium?"

She looked at him innocently and said, "Illinois or Illinois State?"

Rockey's jaw hit the floor. "What?" he mumbled.

She calmly looked at him and stated, "Sir, you are in Bloomington, *Illinois*."

At that moment our pilot was crashing back through the door toward the plane on the tarmac. Adderley and I looked at each other and started to roar with laughter. Rockey started to laugh, too. He began apologizing to the lady at the rental desk. He turned the car he'd just rented back in, and explained he thought he was in Bloomington, *Indiana*. She made him grovel just a bit, but smiled and wished us good luck on our way.

By the time we got to the plane, our pilot had one engine started and a new flight plan to the correct Bloomington had been filed. So, off we went. The pilot was mortified. He'd flown to the wrong Bloomington. He apologized continuously from one Bloomington to the other.

We made it to the Wolverines-Hoosiers contest that day. Sure, we were a little late to tape the opening segment, so we did it live with no rehearsal, but Michigan was victorious. It was one of the few times I remember the trip to the game being a bigger event than the game itself.

And, by the way, the airport in Bloomington, Indiana, had our car rental agreement ready and waiting for us.

Larry Adderley and Jim Brandstatter, safely back from Bloomington.

"Move the Ball or Move the Body..."

Back in the days of Fritz Crisler, Michigan enjoyed football success that rivaled the days when Fielding Yost was working the sidelines. Crisler was a taskmaster, but he also helped shape the game. It was under Crisler's watch that the width of the goalposts was standardized, and it was Crisler who designed the famous winged helmet for Michigan. His toughness also became one of his trademarks.

Albert "The Ox" Wistert remembers Crisler's toughness in an incident at practice one day at Ferry Field during Wistert's sophomore year. "Fritz always said, 'Put ankle wraps on, fellas, to protect your ankles,'" Wistert said. "Well, one day I was late for practice, and I didn't have time to put my ankle wraps on, so I went out and scrimmaged. Wouldn't you know it, I broke an ankle."

Wistert remembers the trainer coming over and removing his shoe and sock. He was in considerable pain. "Fritz was standing right over me as the trainer was working, and when he saw I had no ankle wraps on, Fritz said, 'Where are your ankle wraps, Wistert?'" Al then explained through the pain that he had been late and didn't have time to wrap his ankles. According to Wistert, Fritz growled at him, "Serves you right."

Fritz then turned away and yelled to the rest of the team, "Well, let's move the ball or move the body, I don't want to waste any more time here."

Yost the Teacher

LaVerne "Kip" Taylor played at Michigan and scored the first touchdown at Michigan Stadium in 1927. While Fielding H. Yost had just retired the season before, he was still watching over the football program and the players.

Kip Taylor remembers him well, and he remembers that even though Yost wasn't coaching he was still teaching the game. During a practice one day at a brand new Michigan Stadium, Yost gathered the team around him and pointed down between his feet at the goal line. According to Taylor, Yost looked at them. "You know what that is?" he asked. "Yes, that's the goal line," the team responded.

"The old man then stepped over the goal line," Taylor remembers, "and then he stepped back. He stepped over again, and he stepped back. I bet he did that 20 times. We all thought, 'Geez, this guy is off his rocker.'"

Taylor says Yost then took a long pause for effect, while looking at each of them, kind of waiting for an answer. The team got quiet, and Yost finally said, "Don't you know, I could step over this goal line all day and all night, and it won't count a damn thing if I don't have that little brown thing under my arm."

"I never forgot that," Taylor says. "That was his way of telling you to hang on to the damn ball if you go over that goal line, because it isn't going to count if you haven't got the ball!"

Fielding Yost the teacher.

Make 'em, Now Break 'em

Rivalries are developed over years. There are a lot of factors that go into a rivalry, and one of them can be geographical. Take, for instance, the Michigan vs. Michigan State rivalry. The two schools are located 60 miles apart. Both universities recruit from the same talent pool. Both play in the Big Ten Conference. They meet every year on the gridiron. It is the perfect environment for developing a rivalry.

Coaches have a way of getting a team ready for a rivalry game, and Fritz Crisler was one of the best. Before a Wolverine-Spartan matchup one Saturday at Michigan Stadium, Crisler wanted to get his team fired up. Al Wistert was a young player on the Michigan team, and he remembers the pregame pep talk very well.

"Fritz got us all together in the locker room," Wistert recalls, and Crisler said, "You know Michigan State? Nobody ever heard about Michigan State until they beat us." Wistert remembers Fritz letting that sink in for a moment, then stopping and shouting, "So you guys made 'em. Now I want you to go out there today and break 'em!"

According to Wistert, Fritz's pregame talk worked, as the Wolverines went out that day and broke the Spartans.

M vs. OSU Pregame 1969: Truth or Fiction?

There are a lot of stories that circulate about fiery pregame talks, or ranting and raving halftime speeches from coaches, that are sometimes blown out of proportion. Such is the case with Bo Schembechler's pregame talk to his team before the Ohio State game at Michigan Stadium in 1969.

The 24-12 Michigan win was one of the Wolverines' greatest triumphs over the No. 1-ranked and unbeaten Buckeyes. It came a year after Ohio State humbled Michigan 50-14 in Columbus. The rumors were that Bo played up the previous year's score and revved the team to such a fever pitch that we broke chairs and tore the door off the locker room before we headed down the tunnel to the field.

Here is the real story. I know. I was there.

During the week prior to the game, the scout team players wore white jerseys with scarlet numbers, like Ohio State's away jerseys. The jerseys also had the score 50-14 stenciled just below the throat on the front collar. The staff said nothing about the previous year's score. The reminder on the scout team jerseys was subtle, but the message was clear.

We had a great week of practice and were confident we could win, even though very few gave us any chance. In the locker room before the game there was a heightened sense of emotion, because we all knew this was huge. We were confident, not frightened.

Don Moorehead (No. 27) scores against the Buckeyes in the 1969 classic.

Photo courtesy of Bentley Historical Library, University of Michigan

When Bo addressed us prior to going out for the kickoff, he was serious and very much in control. He matter-of-factly looked at Henry Hill, our middle guard, and said, "Henry, is Jim Stillwagon [Ohio State's middle guard] better than you?" He then looked at Don Moorhead, our quarterback, and said, "Hey Moorhead, is Rex Kern [Ohio State's quarterback] better than you?"

Bo continued this line of questioning to about three or four more guys, asking if their Ohio State counterparts were better players. Of course the answer was an emphatic, "No!"

Bo had made his point. He didn't need to get loud to make it. At that point he raised his voice a little and said, "Men, if we play the way we are capable, if we don't turn the ball over, if we don't miss assignments, if we play hard and execute the fundamentals, *we will win this game.*" After a moment of thoughtful silence, Bo shouted, "*Now, let's go out and win!*"

The idea that a pregame, rah-rah speech can make a difference was never a Schembechler characteristic. "If you want to motivate, to stimulate," Bo says, "it may come during the week. It may have come before you left the hotel to come to the locker room to dress. These speeches come from time to time when you think they are necessary."

Against Ohio State that November Saturday in 1969, it wasn't necessary. "There's no such thing as the ol' pregame/halftime, Let's Go Win One for the Gipper speech. At least not in my judgment," Bo concluded.

Based on what I know of that locker room before the 1969 Ohio State game, I believe Bo. He knew he didn't need to fire us up emotionally; we were already at an emotional peak. Bo wanted us to be focused on the job at hand. He was quiet but intense.

So remember, truth and fiction. The fiction makes a better story, but the truth is, Jim Mandich, our captain, did not rip the locker room door off its hinges. We didn't throw chairs against the walls, or break anything. All we did was *win!*

"I Fumbled the Ball!"

You would think that asking the second all-time leading ground-gainer in Michigan football history what some of his favorite moments in Michigan Stadium were, you wouldn't get a terse, "I fumbled the ball."

Of course I'm talking about Jamie Morris, who held the record for the most rushing yards in a career until Anthony Thomas came along in 2000 and broke it. Still, I was surprised by Jamie's response, and said, "What are you talking about?"

"I was the guy who fumbled the ball in 1984 when Harbaugh broke his arm," Jamie said.

Right away, I understood the significance of fumbling that ball. Quarterback Jim Harbaugh was lost for the season when he broke his arm trying to recover the Morris fumble. The Wolverines went on to their worst year ever under Bo Schembechler, finishing the season with a 6-6 record. The Harbaugh injury was a key factor in the 1984 slide, and Jamie Morris has been bearing the pain of that ever since.

What made it worse was that the fumble came against archrival Michigan State, and the Wolverines lost the game to boot. Talk about a double dip. Jamie Morris had to weather some real adversity. "You're talking about a kid who came from Massachusetts, who has only seen a Michigan-Michigan State game from afar, who really didn't understand the magnitude of it," Jamie remembers.

"That game is brother against brother," Morris recalls. "I did not understand the magnitude until that fumble. I don't want to say it caused our spiral down that year, but we lost our starting quarterback, and I fumbled the ball on that play."

It's funny how some things stay with you. Here is a guy who was responsible, in part, for a whole host of victories at Michigan Stadium. Yet Jamie Morris remembers the fumble that cost his team. That fumble happened in his freshman year. Jamie went on to cover himself in glory after that fumble. Jim Harbaugh recovered from his broken arm, became an All-American, and followed it up with a very successful run in the NFL.

Even Schembechler, when asked about Jamie's career, doesn't recall the fumble against Michigan State. Bo prefers to remember his evaluation of what Morris could become when he arrived at Michigan as a freshman. "Here's a kid who I thought would be a very fine kick-return specialist," Bo says with a laugh, "and he ended up becoming the all-time leading ground-gainer in Michigan history. What do you know about that!"

So, next time you see Jamie Morris around Ann Arbor, tell him not to worry, we forgive him for the fumble. He's made up for it a hundred times over.

I Wanted My Letter

There was a time in Michigan football when varsity letters were awarded only if you had played the requisite number of minutes in games. You were awarded your varsity "M" only if you met these minutes requirements. That policy changed not long after Bo Schembechler arrived in Ann Arbor in 1969. As we understand it, Bo went to Don Canham and told him that every player who came out to practice every day during the course of the season and contributed to the team in whatever capacity deserved a letter. Canham agreed, and the policy changed.

Before Schembechler arrived, though, players were very aware of the minutes they played. One of those players, in the mid-1960s, was Tom Parkhill.

"The highlight for me in a couple of those years was making the travel squad. There was one year," Parkhill laughs, "where my job on the travel squad to Ohio State wasn't on the bench. You know we only traveled 44 guys in those days. Anyway, I was assigned as a spotter in the press box for Bob Ufer.

"Now I want you to know," Parky remembers, "I didn't say a word during that broadcast. Ufer did all the talking. We beat Ohio State 10-0. I enjoyed the game in the warmth of the press box.

"But really, I only got in games when we had a big lead," Parkhill says, "and because of the policy that varsity letters were awarded on the basis of minutes played, I made up my mind I had to figure out a way to get out there on that field. I was the backup holder on extra points and field goals for Timberlake and Sygar. I tried to make a deal with Timberlake to let me hold for a couple of kicks so I could get my minutes for my letter.

"Luckily, I got my letter," Parky recalls. "But, my moment at Michigan Stadium came when we had a big lead against Wisconsin. Head coach Bump Elliott basically put the fourth team in. The last thing he said to us before we went in was, 'Hey, whatever you do, don't throw the ball.' Pete Hollis was the quarterback," Parkhill now laughs, "and he had other ideas. Pete immediately called, Left 72, Flag Pattern.

"Believe it or not," Parkhill recalls, "with my lightning speed, I sat the defensive back on his butt, broke into the end zone, the ball was thrown, and I dropped it.

"Now when we have our reunions," Parky says, "The only thing the guys remember is me dropping that pass. Rowser and Yearby and those guys can't forget the dropped pass. They may kid me about it, but I did win my letter."

The First TD

In 1926, "Kip" Taylor enrolled at the University of Michigan. He also played football and came to the Wolverine squad as a halfback. "They said to me, you don't have enough speed for a halfback," Taylor remembers. "So they moved me to an end. Hell, I didn't know anything about end play."

Kip Taylor, the first ever in the end zone.

By 1927, Taylor had a little better working knowledge of the end position, and he was starting on the Michigan football team. It was also in 1927 when the construction of Michigan Stadium was completed. On October 1, the Wolverines played their first game in their new home, and Kip Taylor was on their No.1 offensive unit.

"I was at the right end, and Bennie Oosterbaan was at the left," Taylor recalls. "We were trying to hit Oosterbaan with all the passes, and naturally, that's right, because he was a great receiver. One of the finest athletes I've ever known, and a great friend.

"But," Taylor went on, "I was running around with no passes coming my way, and one time I came back to the huddle with my tongue hanging out and I said, "'Throw the goddamn ball at me, I'm wide open.'"

"Shut up, you sophomore!" was the answer Taylor received from his senior teammates.

"So I shut up. About three plays later, Louie Gilbert, who was an All-America halfback, called the same pass play," Taylor remembers it as if it were yesterday. "The right end was supposed to run diagonally down the field, and the other end was supposed to cut underneath him. So, they snap the ball, and I run down thinking all I have to do is keep my man off the other end. I looked up as an afterthought, and there is the goddamn ball. So I caught it, and since I played halfback in high school, I figured I better run toward the goal. I stiff-armed one guy, sidestepped another, and went in to score.

"I had no idea it was No. 1," Taylor laughs. "My dad was in the bleachers, and I think I can still hear him yelling."

There have been a lot of people yelling after Michigan touchdowns since that afternoon in 1927, but none of them have the distinction of being the first. That belongs solely to Kip Taylor.

Kip Taylor never scored again for Michigan. Three games into that season he broke a bone in his neck and never played again. "Hell, they wouldn't let me play tiddly-winks after that," Taylor said.

Whether he played another down or not, Kip Taylor remains forever in the record books at Michigan as the first man to score a touchdown in the storied history of Michigan Stadium.

The Colorado Prayer

One of the most infamous moments in Michigan Stadium history came in late September 1994. The University of Colorado was trailing Michigan in the closing seconds, 26-21. Colorado had one last chance, a Hail Mary pass from about 60 yards away from the Wolverine goal line. Incredibly, Kordell Stewart threw a 65-yard pass, and Michael Westbrook caught the tipped ball to give Colorado a heart-stopping win, 27-26.

How could it happen? Well, Michigan defensive back Chuck Winters was right in the middle of the play. "The first thing you've got to remember was that at the end of the first half, they ran the very same play, and I intercepted it," Winters recalls. "So we *knew* that Stewart could throw it that far."

"The key at the end of the game," Winters remembers, "all of our underneath guys missed jamming the receivers at the line of scrimmage. So, I'm backing up, and we've got Westbrook, Carruth, and another guy coming down on us. I'm running with the third guy, and I've got him covered. Ty Law is running with Westbrook and he's trailing by just a little. When the ball goes up, we're all in position, and Ty tries to intercept it. As we jumped, both of us got hit in the legs and thrown off balance. The ball bounced off Ty's shoulder pads, and as I'm falling, I can see Westbrook right behind me catching the ball.

"That was the worst feeling in the world right there," said Winters. "We were just sick. It took me at least two weeks to get over it. It was on television every day. I mean, the coaches were talking about it. We saw videotape of it, man, that was the worst feeling in the world."

Winters remembers the sense of shock in the locker room after the game, "It was like, 'This didn't really happen, did it?' We all just sat around and looked at each other like, 'Man, did this really just happen?'"

Chuck Winters (No. 35) makes a tackle against Colorado.

Sadly for the Wolverines, it did happen. For Chuck Winters, it is a memory that stays with him, because he was right there in the middle of it and still can't change the bounce of the ball, no matter how many times he replays it.

"I look back at it now," Winters says, "and I see that I'm part of history, only I don't want to be part of *that* history."

Passing the Broadcast Torch

One of the great names in Michigan football history never played a down in the winged helmet, but if you are going to write a book called *Tales from Michigan Stadium*, you had better include the name of Bob Ufer.

Bob Ufer broadcast 362 straight Michigan games in a career that spanned 37 years. He is, to this day, a legendary figure around Ann Arbor. He was an All-American at Michigan in track as a student-athlete, and his love for Michigan was complete. There was great sadness in 1981 when Bob was stricken with cancer, and his broadcasts of Michigan football were coming to an end.

The man who had the unenviable task of taking over for Bob as the play-by-play voice of Michigan football would be WJR Radio broadcaster Frank Beckmann. When Ufer's health caused him to finally relinquish his spot behind the microphone, Frank was ready, but more importantly, Bob was very gracious and extremely helpful in passing the torch to his successor.

"The biggest thing that I remember," says Beckmann, "is how big a help he was. Instead of being a guy who felt sorry for himself, he was more interested in making sure that Michigan football broadcasts continued to sound good. So he went out of his way to help me in any way he could."

Beckmann feels Bob really became the ultimate Michigan man in those final days. He was a team guy right to the end. During his final broadcasts, Bob's doctors advised his not to work the entire game as the play-by-play guy. They felt it would be too much, given the difficult treatments he was undergoing for his cancer. However, the doctors did give him the green light to work the pregame radio show.

"He would do the pregame and then leave, I think for two reasons," Beckmann recalls. "One, he would miss it so much, and two, he didn't want to put any pressure on me. He didn't want me to feel his presence, as if he was watching over me. He made it so easy for me. It was amazing."

Bob's handling of the situation is something Beckmann will never forget. "He was one of the great people in Michigan history. You know, you hear stories of the legendary names in Michigan history," Beckmann continues, "how they are selfless and how they care about the school more than themselves. Well, Ufer epitomized it."

Bob was one of a kind. Michigan Stadium was his home on fall Saturdays for 37 years. The great stadium at the corner of Main and Stadium has seen a lot in its day, but it will never see another like Bob Ufer.

Photo by Per H. Kjeldsen

The one and only Bob Ufer.

The Highest-Paid Color Announcer in History

Sitting in the broadcast booth at Michigan Stadium, the memories of Bob Ufer's calls of Michigan football are almost as important as some of the plays that happened there. Bob's style was unique in his broadcasts from the "hole that Yost dug, Canham carpeted, and Schembechler filled every Saturday," to borrow a Ufer phrase.

Some folks might not remember, but Bob always had color commentators with him during broadcasts. You didn't hear much from them, because Bob dominated a broadcast. Nobody really cared, even the color commentators, because Bob was so good.

One of those color men was former Michigan great Don Lund. "Lundo," as he is affectionately called, says working a game with Bob was a snap. "I guess you could call me a color man," Lundo recalls. "Bob Foreman (Michigan's former Alumni Association director) once told me, 'Lundo, you must be the highest-paid color man in history, you get a chance to say two words a broadcast.'"

Lund laughs about the times Bob would get wound up as his Wolverines were charging toward another victory. "There were times when stat man Jack Lane and I would look at each other during a particularly exciting part of a game," Lund chuckles, "and Bob would be going a mile a minute. In his later years, his eyesight was not as good as it once was, and in some games, Lane and I looked at each other wondering if Bob was watching the same game we were.

"He was Maize and Blue through and through," remembers Lund, "and great for Michigan."

He was indeed, and whatever game Bob Ufer watched and related to all of us was the game we all wanted to hear.

"It Wasn't My Fault!"

Michigan Stadium is very impressive when it's full, and it can be very ominous when it's empty. It happened to be empty for one of my most interesting moments with Bo Schembechler.

It was early in the fall of 1969, Bo's first year at Michigan, and we had to practice in the Stadium. It was the first year of the new artificial surface, "Tartan Turf," in the Stadium. They put the surface down first so that we were ready for the season, but the practice field hadn't been finished by the time the season started. So every day for practice in the early fall, we would dress in Yost Field House and walk to the Stadium across the practice fields and train tracks, through the parking lot and down the tunnel onto the Michigan Stadium field.

This particular Tuesday was after we had lost 40-17 to Missouri the Saturday before. During the game, Missouri had blocked a punt. It was a cardinal sin for a Bo Schembechler-coached team to have a punt blocked, so as we marched into the Stadium that day for practice, we knew it would be a rough one.

At the time, I was the backup to Dan Dierdorf at strong tackle. Dan had suffered a hip-pointer in the game and was unable to practice that day, so I was running with the first team. Just a sophomore, I was as nervous as you can imagine to be filling in for an All-American, and the last thing I wanted to do was screw up.

One of the first things we did that day after warming up was go to a special teams session, and the first part of special teams drills was the punt team. I got in the huddle with the first team and was ready to go. Before we ran the first play against the punt-block unit, Bo went to their huddle and said, loudly enough for everyone to hear, "I want you guys to block this punt. Go hard, and the guy that blocks one, I'll buy him a milk shake!"

So we lined up, the ball was snapped and I carried out my assignment correctly, knocking two guys off stride who had tried to get through the outside gap between the tight end and me. I then released to go downfield and cover the punt. About 15 yards downfield I looked up to locate the ball. *There was no ball! The punt had been blocked!*

The next thing I heard was a bellowing Schembechler, yelling from behind me, some 40 yards away, "You dumb son of a..."

I peeled off on my punt coverage and took a wide turn back to the huddle thinking to myself, "Oh man, somebody is in big trouble."

As I caught sight of Bo, he was running and flailing his arms while screaming more bad things about some poor guy who had missed a block. As I ran, I noticed he kept changing direction and was in a direct course to intercept me.

Now you've got to understand, in an empty Michigan Stadium, the sound of his voice reverberated and was amplified as if he were screaming in the cavernous confines of St. Peter's Basilica. Everyone at practice stopped and watched.

In the frenzied moments when I finally realized that I was his target, the entire play flashed before my eyes. I had done everything right; why was he yelling at me?

At about that time, he left his feet about a yard away from me and grabbed me by the shoulder pads and shook me. For the life of me I can't remember what he said. I can only guess that I was in a state of shock and was incapable of feeling anything. I was told he called me a number of names. He said I was the worst tackle in the history of intercollegiate football, and that I would never play at Michigan. The one thing he said that I did remember was, "Leave! Get out of here!"

He then turned around and headed back to the huddle for the next punt. I stood there for a moment not sure what to do. Finally, as I was hyperventilating in fear and shock, I turned to walk up the tunnel and out of the Stadium. My career was over.

I never got to the tunnel. My position coach, Jerry Hanlon, caught me, grabbed me by the arm, and pulled me back toward practice. Near tears, I asked him, "What's going on?"

He said, "C'mon, it wasn't your fault."

As the blood returned to my brain, I said, "What? Did you tell him?"

"No," Jerry responded, "I'll tell him later."

Still in a state of semi-shock, I went back to practice and completed the day. Every time we were in a huddle and Bo was in the middle, I kept thinking he'd notice and kick me out again, but he never did.

After practice, all of the guys came up and patted me on the back and told me not to worry. They all thought it was a great show. They got a good laugh out of it.

For the rest of the week, nothing was ever said about it. Coach Hanlon had told me not to worry, I had done the right thing and ought to keep up the good work.

It wasn't until Friday of that week when Bo and I settled the issue. It was at training table. I was filing through the cafeteria line at South Quad getting dinner, and he was waiting at the end of the line. As I got to him, he said, "You don't think it was your fault, do you?" It was four days removed, but I knew exactly what he was talking about, and I said, "No."

Bo smiled, which to be honest, shocked me a little and said, "Yeah, you're probably right, but you know, your split with the guard may have been a little too wide. Watch that the next time."

He then turned and went to eat with the other coaches. I stood there for a moment and suddenly everything was all right. I truly felt part of the team. Call it my red badge of courage. It's hard to explain, but at that moment I'd have run through a wall for Bo and still will to this day if he wants me to.

By the way, the two guys who made the mistake and allowed the punt to be blocked that day were two seniors: the right guard and the fullback. Their names shall not be mentioned here, to protect the guilty. They are also good friends who remain two of my favorite people.

*James Hall (No. 56) gets under the regular
"Go Blue" banner with no trouble.*

They Stole the Banner

Some events that players remember at Michigan Stadium don't necessarily have anything to do with plays in a game. In the case of James Hall, a defensive end who played on the national championship team of 1997, an event *before* a game keeps him chuckling to this very day.

"The year we played Syracuse in The Big House," James recalls, "somebody stole the M-Club Go Blue banner, so they brought out this makeshift banner. It was extremely high, you know, much higher than the usual banner.

"So as we ran out for the game, all excited, everybody wanted to jump up and touch the banner. So, the first wave of guys tried to jump up and touch it, but when they realized they couldn't reach it, they lost balance and fell on the field," Hall recalls with a laugh.

"That was one of the funniest things," Hall remembers. "I mean, sometimes a guy would fall trying to touch it, but that banner was so high, and if a guy did touch it, it was so stiff, much more than the other banner, the guy's legs would fly out from under him and he'd fall. That was hilarious to me. It was one of the funniest moments I can remember."

"We Set a Record, But Couldn't Claim It!"

One of the great names in Michigan history is former athletic director Don Canham. It was said that the smartest thing Canham did in his tenure at Michigan was hire football coach Bo Schembechler. Don would readily agree to that, but he did so much more. To suggest that bringing Bo to Ann Arbor was his only triumph is completely inaccurate and does a disservice to this legendary Michigan man.

One of his great accomplishments was marketing Michigan football to the fans. He created an atmosphere that made Michigan Stadium an all-day party location on a football Saturday, and soon after he took over, the Wolverines began selling out every game with over 100,000 faithful showing up.

There was one instance, though, when he got more fans than he bargained for.

"I'll give you a good story," Canham told me recently. "It involved a Purdue game. We had a guy who was active in the Cub Scouts, and he printed all of our football tickets at that time. We told him that our Homecoming game that year was with Northwestern and that he could bring his Cub Scouts to that game. We figured we would get maybe 60,000 for Northwestern, so we could handle the Cub Scouts.

"Well," Canham laughed as he recalled the mix-up, "the guy printed the Homecoming tickets for the Purdue game, and they had a hot team. We had a sell-out situation, and 9,000 Cub Scouts showed up. So, I got a hold of Bob Flora, our stadium guy, and told him we had a big mess here.

"Flora already knew something was wrong," Canham chuckled. "He said, 'What's going on, where are all the Cub Scouts coming from?'"

At that point, Canham says, they had to act quickly. "I told Flora, "OK, get some people, spread the Cub Scouts all over the Stadium, put them in the aisles, sit them on people's laps, whatever, and he did. We set an attendance record of 109,000 that day, and the damn thing was, *we couldn't claim it!*"

"What Time Are We Leaving?"

One of the little-known facts about Don Canham is that he very rarely saw a complete football game at Michigan Stadium.

As a former track coach at Michigan, and a darn good one, you would have thought that Canham could handle the stress of the big game. That isn't altogether true.

"I used to walk out of this place all the time just after the game started," Canham says. "Elroy Hirsch, the athletic director of Wisconsin, used to come up to me before our game and say, 'Canham, what time are we leaving?' And we'd drive out to my factory and watch the game on television."

It doesn't seem like this is the kind of thing you'd expect out of Don Canham, but those were different times back then, and Canham was nervous. "I was so nervous," he admits, "I'd hang around and meet everybody before the game, but sometime in the first quarter I would have to leave the Stadium, because you see, I knew all the injuries and that stuff, and I knew how important one game was. In those days, you know, we were fighting for our lives, financially! I mean, if we made a bowl game, boy, that was gravy, and we could only make one bowl game. So, there were times when I didn't see much of the season."

The Diminutive Left-Hander

In his first six years at the helm of Michigan football, Bo Schembechler had a great run. He had become one of the top coaches in the country, but entering his seventh year, the program faced changes. Freshmen were now allowed to compete at the varsity level. With the graduation of Dennis Franklin, Bo needed a quarterback to direct his option attack. The only one he had was an incoming freshman from Flint, Michigan, named Rick Leach.

Would Bo start a freshman quarterback? It didn't seem likely, but Leach was a different story. Rick was a confident young man. "I told my dad after I signed my scholarship, after I had been in Ann Arbor working out, that I was gonna do it," Leach remembers. "I told him I was gonna pull it off. My dad, at the time, said he didn't want to burst my bubble, but he told me it might be too much to bite off, even though he was pleased with my confidence.

"When I got to Michigan and evaluated the situation at quarterback at the time," Leach recalls, "it was wide open. I thought I would have a good opportunity to be a backup based on what we had, and if certain things happened, you never know."

In the meantime, there was a difference of opinion on the coach's staff.

"There was quite a controversy on our staff," Schembechler remembers, "whether we go with a veteran quarterback or whether we take this new, young, snot-nosed freshman and expose him immediately. The general consensus was to go with the veteran. However, I felt if we were so close that we had to argue over who the quarterback was, that in the next four years, this kid Leach was gonna be pretty decent. So, we might as well get into it right now."

As head coach, Bo's opinion carried the day. He also held back on officially telling anyone about his decision until very late. Leach wasn't sure he was going to start that first game on the road at Wisconsin until they had arrived in Madison. "Bo never told me officially until Friday afternoon working out in their stadium," Leach remembers. "I don't think he told me because he didn't want things to get more out of hand than they already were. He knew how nervous I was going to be, and he probably didn't want to put more on my plate than I could handle."

Schembechler handled it very delicately, but he also told Leach something that made it easier on Rick to put the outside pressure in perspective. "I'll always remember what he told me prior to that game. He said, 'Look, here at Michigan the quarterback is going to get more praise than he deserves when things are going well and he's going to take more heat than he should when things don't go well. I'm telling you that now, and I want you to remember what I say next and never forget it. The only guy you've got to keep happy here is *me*. If things go south, I'll protect you. Just remember, you don't have to worry about what anybody says except me.'"

Leach certainly pleased Bo well enough. Rick went on to start 48 straight games at quarterback. He posted a record of 38-8-2 as the starter. The Wolverines won three Big Ten titles over that period and appeared in four bowl games with Leach at quarterback.

Despite Leach's glowing record, there were some tough moments. In that first year, after an opening win at Wisconsin, Michigan tied their next two games against Stanford and Baylor. Some folks were getting restless, and Leach felt the first sting of criticism. "I remember walking across campus one time, and seeing people laughing and giggling at me. I had no idea what was going on until I picked up the *Michigan Daily*." Leach chuckles about it now, but at the time, it was a difficult lesson. "The paper had run a cartoon of a blind guy with a cane wearing glasses, and they were already calling for my head, saying we could never win with me as a quarterback. It was funny, because I was ticked off, frustrated, and angry. I was doing everything in my power to win. And, it wasn't like we got beat. We had tied a couple of games. And I'll never forget walking into my quarterback meeting that day; Bo asked me how I was doing. I said, well, there are a few things going on that I'm not too happy about. With that, he laid the article down in front of me and asked if that was what I was talking about.

"He got a kick out of it," Leach says today. "He started laughing, and I felt better almost immediately." The very next Saturday

Bo and Rick Leach, side by side through 38 wins.

in Michigan Stadium, Rick played a great game in helping the Wolverines to a 31-7 win over Missouri.

Through the years, Leach remains one of Bo's favorites. Schembechler even has a unique nickname for Rick. He calls Leach "The Diminutive Left-Hander." Bo loves nicknames, and for Rick, it goes back to those days when he was a freshman. "I think he took a shine to me right when I got to Michigan," Leach says. "Being left-handed himself and playing so early in my career, there was a bond there that very few players had. It was mainly due to the fact that all my meetings, all my film work, all the strategy sessions were done sitting down with Bo. You know, I had a unique relationship with him that I treasured when I was there. I treasured it when I was in professional athletics, and I treasure it even more now."

The Pylon Was Missing

Jon Falk has been the equipment manager for Michigan football since 1973. There isn't anyone who knows more of the untold secrets of Michigan Stadium than Jon Falk.

One of those stories comes from the 1975 game against Baylor that Michigan tied 14-14. "I came out at the half," Jon remembers, "and we had kicked off with a 14-7 lead. One of the kids on the sideline came running over to me and told me that the pylon in the corner of the north end zone at the goal line was missing. Well, Baylor started to move the ball on us, heading toward that goal line. I had to do something, so I ran across the field and up the tunnel to a little storage area where we kept extra pylons.

"Once I got the pylon, I ran back down the tunnel, and I'm running toward the goal line to get the pylon placed at the goal line. Now Baylor, you understand, has moved the ball close to our end zone, and they are moving in to score. As I'm running down the sideline with the pylon in my hand, the fullback from Baylor gets pushed out at the goal line. The referee looks down, doesn't see the pylon, and waves it off, no touchdown. We held them at the goal line. As soon as he left, I ran over and set the pylon on the field. The ref looked at me like, 'Hey, what's going on here?' I told him I was sorry."

The game continued on, ended in a tie, and Jon thought that was the end of it until he got some mail from Dallas. "Somebody sent me an article from a newspaper," Jon says, "and the article was from the day after the game. Grant Teaff, the head coach at Baylor, was quoted as saying that when his coaches watched the film, they saw me running down the sideline with the pylon in my hand trying to get that pylon set. Teaff apparently noticed the pylon was not there, but said, "I've got nothing against Michigan. I saw the kid on the film, and he was making an honest effort to get the pylon set, but he just didn't get there in time.' I was that kid," Jon laughs today.

"I was trying to get over there as fast as I could," Jon adds, "I wasn't trying to cheat anybody. I just couldn't make it fast enough."

We might add that since that game, the pylons are always checked and in place before every Michigan game in Ann Arbor.

Jon Falk roaming the Michigan sideline, with all pylons in place.

It's a Wonderful Place to Play

One of the legendary names in Michigan football history is Ron Kramer. His number, 87, is one of only five numbers that has been retired, so you know that Ron Kramer's shadow is large around Ann Arbor.

Ron is also a bit of a character. A delightful character certainly, but he marches to a bit of a different drummer. I affectionately call him "The Legend," and he has never discouraged me. He is a great source of information and history about Michigan, and some of it never made the sports pages when he was the Wolverines' main man in the 1950s.

One of the tales he related to me had Michigan Stadium as one central character and his teammate-roommate, who shall remain nameless, as the other. The story, though, does not involve a football game. As a matter of fact, this story happened at night. "When I was in school," Kramer started with a chuckle, "they always left the gate open to the Stadium, and we would park there at night with our girlfriends. At 10:30 we had to leave because all the girls had to be in anyway, and they would then lock the gate."

At this point, Ron gets a devilish grin on his face and continues, "One night, my roommate is maybe mushing a little too much, and he gets caught in the Stadium *after* they locked the gate. So he has to get out of the car, climb over the top of the fence, including the barbed wire, walk all the way over to South State Street and wake up one of the Stadium guys, Bob Hurst, to open up the gate. My roomie then drives out of the Stadium and gets his girl back to the dorm, really late. Now, understand," Kramer continues, "the girlfriend gets in so far past curfew, she can't go out on weekends for the next month!"

We aren't done yet, and I know it because Ron begins to relish the finish to this tale. "About four days later, my roommate gets this postcard at the Sigma Chi house," Kramer recalls, "It's a picture of Michigan Stadium. The mail, you know, for both of us, came to the room, and even though it was addressed to him, I was a bit nosey, so, I turned it over and read it.

"It said," Kramer recalls with glee, "'Dear _____, It's a wonderful place to play, isn't it?' And it was signed, 'Coach Bennie Oosterbaan.'"

We Had 1,097 Requests

When Michigan football tees it up for a big game, there are a lot of people who are interested in seeing the action. Part of the problem that The Big House presents is where to put all of the media that request credentials for games. Seating the more than 100,000 spectators is easy. The media and their equipment can be a bit more difficult.

Bruce Madej and his staff have handled the media at Michigan Stadium for years as an associate athletic director and sports information director. He says the biggest media-game day that he can remember came in November 1997 when the Wolverines and Ohio State battled in a game with huge implications. Michigan was playing for an unbeaten season and was ranked No. 1 in the country. They were on their way to a national title, but Ohio State would have liked nothing better than to have spoiled the Wolverines' plans. This grudge match had attracted national attention, so the media buildup was immense, and when game day approached, Bruce Madej was under siege.

"We had 1,097 credentials out for that game," Madej admits. "We had eight live TV shows going on before the game including CNN and ESPN. That day, I literally was almost more concerned about parking satellite trucks than I was about what was going to happen in the game. We had satellite trucks parked all the way down Main Street on the south side, lining them up so they could hit their uplinks."

That was the biggest media contingent Bruce had to tolerate, but there were other times when some media didn't get in.

Sometimes you get in the press box, sometimes you don't.

When a game is on the schedule a year in advance and a media outlet waits until the last minute to request a package of credentials, a sports information director at a big program with a big stadium can get a bit impatient and a bit testy. This situation for presented itself to Bruce in the 1991 season. "It was the Florida State game," Bruce recalled.

The Seminoles were ranked No. 1 in the country, and Michigan was ranked No. 3 in the country at the time, so a lot of people were getting revved up for it, and the press requests were flooding the offices all week. Some of them had to be denied, and one late request really had Bruce on edge.

"It was Friday before the game," Madej explains. "Can you imagine, less than 24 hours prior to kickoff, CNN calls. I told them there was no way, not this late. I can't issue them the credentials. At this point I am so ticked off they called so late, having known for more than a year about the game, there was no way they were getting in. I had to call Wayne Hogan, the Florida State sports information director, and explain the situation, just in case he got a call from CNN, he'd know what happened. I told Wayne, I had shut CNN down. I was still miffed they'd call so late, so I related to Wayne what I told them when I shut them down. I said, 'You can go cover the Gulf War, but you are not going to cover Michigan vs. Florida State!'" Wayne got a kick out of that, so he related the story to a guy from *Sports Illustrated*. "Wouldn't you know," Bruce says sheepishly, "*SI* used that quote in a subsequent issue."

I Skipped Out of Bounds

It is interesting that as I talk to former players from Michigan while putting this book together, each one of them has a specific play or memory that has left a lasting impression on them. Such is the case with one of the Wolverines' all-time great running backs, Harlan Huckleby.

"It was in my freshman year," Harlan recalls, "and we were beating somebody. I can't remember who it was, but it was during those years when we beat a lot of teams pretty good. So I get in the game, and as a freshman, you're pretty hyped up. You know, the big stadium, the fans, you are finally out there on the carpet, and you've finally got your chance to shine. Now there are a bunch of us youngsters out there in the same situation. The game is out of reach, and we are all so excited to be out there that we start making mistakes. First, somebody jumps offsides. Then we run a play, but somebody is holding. Then the next play," Huckleby continues, "I jump, and we get a motion call. So I mean it's about third down and forever. Back then a third-and-forever was just as likely to be a run as it was a pass. I don't think we had a pass in the playbook that went as deep as we had to go. So, we finally pull a play off. We come down the line on the option, and it's on our sideline too. Rick [Leach] comes down to the end, pitches it to me, and *swoosh*, I am running right up the chute, it is perfect!

"I am in the clear, and it looks good for about 20 or 30 yards. And then, I don't know what came over me," Harlan remembers. "As a couple of defenders are coming at me from the side, I do a little Joe Washington-like skip out of bounds. I didn't lower the shoulder and take on the tacklers. I just skipped out of bounds. It was a nice run and I'm feeling pretty good; I showed the crowd my speed, but where I went out of bounds was just short of a first down."

Harlan says he remembers the next sequence of events as if it were yesterday. "As I start walking up the sideline back toward the middle of our bench, I notice there are people getting out of my way. I can't figure that out, and I am a little mixed up. I thought I would have guys patting me on the back after such a good play.

"Huck" roars through a big hole.

I'm thinking I am pretty big stuff. But what it is, people are getting out of the way for Bo, because he is coming down the sideline looking for *me*.

"He is charging," Huckleby remembers. "Now remember, the game is over, we've won it, we are well ahead, but Bo's freshman running back, the so-called 'big-time' young running back, who just broke a big run, has stepped out of bounds before he got to the first-down marker. Oh man," Harlan groans, "Bo is in my face like you would not believe. Trust me when I say this, I never forgot what he told me that afternoon on that sideline in Michigan Stadium.

"I don't ever think, including my professional career, I ever stepped out of bounds ever again. In practice, whatever, I never did that again." Harlan is adamant about the lesson he learned that day. "I'm serious, until the last carry of the last game in my professional career, I never stepped out of bounds on purpose again."

A Magnificent Upset

Many longtime observers of Michigan football argue about the greatest plays, greatest performances and greatest games ever in Michigan Stadium, and there is never a winner in these arguments because everyone has their own special memory. That is how it should be. But I think there is one game that would probably make everyone's top-five list, and that is Michigan's upset of top-ranked Ohio State in 1969.

If you wonder about how that game affected Michigan and its future, all you have to do is hear the impact it had on the principals, like Wolverine rookie coach, Bo Schembechler. "Nobody knew who we were, or what we were doing when we came up here to Michigan," Bo says about his hiring by Don Canham. "Now, they *knew* Michigan. It wasn't like that win put Michigan on the map, but it certainly put *our program* on the map. I mean, there weren't many people out there who knew anything about Schembechler. It certainly wasn't a household word!

"By beating Ohio State, and you've got to get the picture here," Bo relates, "many people said Ohio State was the greatest college football team of all time! The only team the experts said that could give Ohio State a game, at that time, were the Minnesota Vikings! They must have been the hot shots in the NFL then, because that's the way it was. So, beating Ohio, I mean, this was unheard of.

"As our score against Ohio State was being broadcast on all the public address systems in every stadium across this country, can you imagine the football fans and what they were thinking?" Bo lowers his voice now for effect. "'This was no ordinary game. This was a magnificent upset!'"

It wasn't just Bo who felt that way. As a player in that game, I can tell you that to a man, we knew we had a shot at beating Ohio State well before kickoff. Nobody else gave us a chance, but we honestly believed. Longtime Schembechler assistant coach Jerry Hanlon also believed. "Even though the expectations weren't very high when the Miami of Ohio mafia came to Ann Arbor, when we started to win, even our own expectations grew, and we started to put pressure on ourselves. I particularly felt we had a great shot at beating Ohio State the week before we played them," said Hanlon.

What gave Jerry that confidence may have been a 51-6 win by his Wolverines at Iowa the Saturday preceding the showdown with the Buckeyes. "We were so emotional after that Iowa win," Hanlon continued, "that if we could keep from killing each other on the practice field that week leading up to Ohio State, we'd have a chance to win. Sitting up in that press box in the coach's booth with the game in hand 24-12 late in the contest, I got one of the nicest feelings I've ever had in my life. It was a feeling of accomplishment, after you had worked so hard and got things turned around, to see it come to fruition like it did in that game was one of my most satisfying moments in coaching."

There is no question that every player and every coach who participated in that game considers it a special moment in their lives. Beyond the players and coaches, though, I have met fans who have that same sense, that they were a part of something very special just by being in attendance at the game.

The bench explodes as time runs out on the 1969 upset of Ohio State.

Schembechler has said that what put the significance of that Michigan victory in perspective for him was a handwritten note he received a few days after the game from Fritz Crisler. "He wrote this letter as he watched the game from his hospital bed," Bo said. "He wrote how proud he was that he was a Michigan man. He wrote how he loved it so that Michigan stood out that day. He wrote how pleased he was that, once again, Michigan had expressed its dominance over college football!"

The Bo Show or No Show

One of the more interesting stories surrounding Michigan football has been the evolution of the coach's television show, *Michigan Replay*. Even though I have cohosted the show since 1980, I was not the guy who got it started. The man who was the first host with Bo Schembechler in 1975 was WXYZ-TV's Larry Adderley.

Bo had done a coach's show prior to 1975 on Channel 4 in Detroit with longtime broadcaster Don Kremer, but it was not called *Michigan Replay*. The current *Michigan Replay* really got its start in 1975 on Channel 7.

The first producer of the show in 1975 was Bob Lipson, and he is still at it to this very day, so we have had some consistency. In many ways, it is a miracle the show even exists. There were a multitude of hurdles to clear in the early going to make it happen.

First of all, the executive director of the University of Michigan Alumni Association at the time, Bob Foreman, was instrumental in getting the show put together and financed. Bo felt a show like this during the season could be a big asset. "I had talked to Frank Broyles at Arkansas," Bo says, "and he said a show like this served two purposes. You can make some money on it, but more importantly, it really promotes your program because you're on TV every week during the season. I presented the idea to Foreman.

"I told Foreman," remembers Bo, "that I didn't want to run all over the country making speeches to make money. Remember, I wasn't making much money here when I started. So we could accomplish that if we had this show and worked out the financing arrangements as Broyles had explained to me."

Bo wanted to stay close to Ann Arbor and focus on the football program instead of taking off on the banquet circuit in the offseason, and this seemed to be a good way to achieve that goal. It was an idea that Foreman agreed with totally. He helped get Michigan alums on board, and a show was ultimately created.

In the beginning stages of development, Bo was asked if he could agree to a format that had been used before in the state. It was a television show that featured Bump Elliott of Michigan and

Duffy Daugherty of Michigan State. That effort had been called *The Bump and Duffy Show*. It covered both schools in one TV program. The concept was brought to Bo for his take, and he bristled at the thought of it. His reply to the TV executives who were trying to push it was, "Look, it's going to be the *Bo show, or no show!*"

Once that got settled, *Michigan Replay* debuted in 1975 on Channel 7 in Detroit with syndication around the state of Michigan. The reason it wasn't called *The Bo Schembechler Show* was strictly from the instincts of Bob Lipson. At the time, Lipson was a director at WXYZ-TV. He took over the producer reins when the show was cleared to go. The title, though, was a question mark. Lipson maintained that the coach's name shouldn't be a part of the title, because if the coach didn't last a long time, you'd be changing titles every time you changed a coach. Additionally, Lipson felt that the show should be about Michigan football and not the coach. Not surprisingly, Bo wholeheartedly agreed, and *Michigan Replay* was born.

In the beginning, it wasn't the well-oiled machine that it is today. As a matter of fact, in the very first show of 1975, following the opening game at Wisconsin in Rick Leach's freshman year, there were a number of glitches. Bob Lipson remembers the glitches fondly today. "Back then, in order for us to use highlights of the game, we had to use silent, double sprocket, 16-millimeter coach's film. All the games weren't on TV like they are today, so we had to use coach's film," Lipson says. "It was shot super-wide, so the players looked like little ants on the field, but the coaches loved it because they could see what every player did on every play.

"We also did the show live at 4 p.m. on Sundays in those days, so for that first show, we edited our film highlights, gave them to our engineer, he hung them on the projector and off we went."

Lipson remembers the next sequence of events with a laugh, "When we call for the first-half highlight package, I notice something isn't right, but I'm not sure what. Then it hit me—the engineer had loaded the film backwards! The projectionist wasn't used to dealing with silent film. Most of his work in the local news department has sound on the film clips, so he probably never noticed that the film was rolling backwards on the air!"

Larry Adderley was hosting that first show and remembers the great care they had taken to make it as easy as possible for the rookie coach. They all wanted everything to go smoothly. "We were moving along all right until the highlights came up," laughs Adderley. "Then came the first Michigan touchdown, and we expected the word WISCONSIN emblazoned across the end zone, but it was spelled NISNOCSIW!"

Adderley says he did some fast talking and explained to the viewers that we had experienced some technical problems. "We knew what was wrong and explained it, and then Bo turned to me and said, 'Yeah, I wondered why Leach was right-handed!'" Adderley recalls with delight.

During the first commercial break, the projectionist re-hung the film properly, and the rest of the show went very well. But the pioneers of *Michigan Replay*, Bob Lipson and Larry Adderley, look back at the first attempt and smile about the mixup to this very day. As Lipson puts it, "It was hysterical."

"*Throw the Ball to* Me!"

One of the greatest plays in the history of Michigan Stadium occurred in 1979 on a Homecoming Saturday against the Hoosiers of Indiana. If you remember that day, it appeared as though Indiana would pull the upset by tying Michigan at 21. As a matter of fact, when Indiana scored late in the game, Hoosier head coach Lee Corso chose to kick the extra point for the tie than go for two and the win. That decision to kick for the tie by Corso set up one of the most memorable finishes the big house has ever seen.

As Michigan started their last-gasp drive to recover the victory, they found themselves on the Indiana 45-yard line with just six seconds to play in the game. The Wolverines were able to put themselves in that spot thanks to fullback Lawrence Reid. He had caught a pass out of the backfield for a minimal gain, but had hurled the ball out of bounds to stop the clock before he was tackled. The ball wound up in Corso's hands on the Hoosier bench. In reality, Reid didn't need to do that, because Michigan still had one timeout left.

What happened next was pure magic. Bo Schembechler remembers the sequence this way, "What it was, was an *in*-route. You see, by this time, we only had one play left. They obviously were going to play a cold zone, and let those defensive backs stay *way* back. The ball *had* to be completed underneath. Now, if you were going to complete the ball underneath three-deep coverage, *who* in the world would you want to catch that ball? Without question you want it to be Anthony Carter. And I know for a fact that Carter went into that huddle and told Wangler, 'Wangs, you throw that ball to *me!*' And that's what Wangler did, and Carter did the rest."

The man in the middle of all of this was quarterback John Wangler. To find out from inside that huddle what *exactly* went on that special Saturday, we went to Wangler. "I will confirm the fact," Wangler says without hesitation, "that Anthony told me as he was leaving the huddle to throw him the ball, and I told him I would!"

Now it gets a little more fun, because John has an interesting take on the entire play and how they pulled it off. "We broke the huddle and went to the line. The irony, though, I bring up to Bo on a regular basis because of the sophistication of our pass offense at the time. I had to fake our off-tackle play to Butch Woolfolk before I threw the pass. You know, we had to hold those linebackers in tight," Wangler laughs with respectful sarcasm. "With six seconds to play and 45 yards to cover, we wanted to make sure they honored the run! So, after we took care of that hard run fake, we ran the 54 Pass Post. They were in a prevent look, which was fortunate for us. I got the ball to Anthony in that open spot, and he did the rest."

Carter remembers it exactly the same way. "I *did* tell Wangs to throw me the ball," recalls Anthony, "and Ralph Clayton looked at me in the huddle like, what is this freshman talking about? But I just had the confidence that I could make something happen."

He did indeed make something happen. After catching the pass in front of the cornerback, Anthony was knocked off balance. He managed to stay on his feet by putting a hand on the ground to maintain his balance. All the while he was running at full speed.

The scoreboard tells of Carter's heroics.

Heading directly at an oncoming safety, Anthony planted his foot and made a 90-degree cut away from the defender. He accelerated out of his cut like a bullet, avoided the defender, and danced into the end zone with his arms raised.

From that point on it was pure bedlam in Michigan Stadium. Fans streamed onto the field. Carter was mobbed by his teammates and a good portion of the crowd after dancing into the end zone with no time left on the clock to rescue the victory 27-21.

Wangler remembers staying with the game, though. "I actually was running down the field to call timeout. I wasn't sure he was going to score. I thought we might be able to call time and kick a field goal." It wasn't needed though, Carter had indeed scored, and the play has turned into a truly legendary moment in Michigan football history.

After the play, in the midst of the bedlam, Carter was under a mass of humanity, and it all became kind of a blur. "I didn't really think about getting mobbed," Anthony says. "Butch Woolfolk, our running back, actually thought about it and began pulling people off of me. He probably saved my life," Carter laughs, "because I was getting tumbled pretty good at the bottom of that pile."

Besides Wangler and Carter, the man most responsible for putting this play into legendary status was broadcaster Bob Ufer. When it happened, Ufer went ballistic in the press box. The "General George Patton, Bo Schembechler" scoring horn was being blown on overload. A few years later on *Michigan Replay* we set his radio call to videotape and it took on a life of its own. "Even though we hadn't heard it at the time," Wangler says today, "the way Ufer called it really immortalized the play."

Two great sequences in the Ufer call of the play that always send chills down my spine are when he literally screams, "John Wangler to Anthony Carter will be heard for another 100 years of Meechigan football." The other sequence is when he talks about Schembechler and Fielding Yost. Ufer said, "Look at Bo Schembechler down on the sidelines. He's looking up to the heavens, to football's Valhalla, and he's saying, thank you, Fielding Yost, thank you."

A.C.

Anthony Carter was a special player at Michigan. The winning TD against Indiana was certainly his most famous moment at Michigan Stadium, but he had many others. Carter is also a young man who is very shy and hesitant to talk about himself or his exploits on the field. There were times after he had been spectacular during a game when he would take refuge in the coach's locker room. He wasn't very comfortable talking about himself to the media. He would say, "Let them talk to my teammates. They deserve the attention as much as I do."

In February 2002, Carter was inducted into the University of Michigan's Hall of Honor and he had to give an acceptance speech. One of his comments during that speech characterized Anthony very well. He had been talking for a few moments when he paused and said, "I've been talking here for about five minutes. During my career here, I probably didn't say more than five words."

Ufer called A.C. "The Human Torpedo."

To get a measure on what a great player Anthony was, you talk to those who witnessed his talents on an everyday basis. A good source for this is Schembechler. "I remember when Anthony came in as a freshman," recalls Bo, "and we were in one of our early practices. We were testing the arms of our quarterbacks, so we had them throwing deep sideline passes. We had them throwing it as far as they could. The receivers were running straight fly routes down the sideline. After a few minutes we noticed something. There was only one receiver in the bunch that these quarterbacks could not overthrow. It was Anthony."

Bo remembers Carter's ability to run down a pass with great joy. "Speed, to Anthony, is: how fast do I *have* to run? Whatever it took," Bo says, "he ran that fast."

Quarterback John Wangler was also impressed with Anthony's uncanny ability as a receiver. Normally, quarterbacks don't try to squeeze passes in to covered receivers, but in Anthony's case, even if he was double-covered, John was comfortable throwing the ball to him. Somehow, Wangler knew Anthony would make the catch.

"Anthony was fast," Wangler says. "He had 4.4 speed in the 40. But what was really amazing was that he had the same 4.4 speed running sideways!"

Carter actually stopped practice one day in his freshman year just by making a catch. That's right, by just making a catch.

Running back Stanley Edwards witnessed the event. "The receivers were running this drill," Edwards recalls. "They were running deep post patterns. Well, on this one play, the ball was thrown behind Anthony. As he was running, he kind of jumped, and I swear, *he stopped his momentum in midair!* He then kind of spun around and caught the ball in his left hand. He landed on his feet, balanced, and took off running again. Everybody in practice just stopped and looked. The whole field got quiet.

"Bo kind of stopped for a moment," Edwards says, "then he smiled ever so slightly, and yelled, 'OK, next play!'"

Carter, for his part, smiles at remarks like these, but doesn't say too much about himself. One of his favorite moments at Michigan Stadium, other than the Indiana catch, came in his very first game at Michigan as a freshman. "The very first game, against Northwestern, when I returned a punt 78 yards for a touchdown stands out for me," says Anthony. "Being a young guy, the first time I ever touched the ball in Michigan Stadium and bringing it back for a touchdown is something I'll always remember."

The ironic twist with Anthony is that despite his shyness, the huge crowds at Michigan Stadium got his adrenaline pumping. A bit uncomfortable around people, this small-town prodigy from Riviera Beach, Florida, found the 100,000 Maize and Blue faithful perfect company. "Playing in front of that many people," says Carter, "was very exciting, and actually helped me get motivated. You know, we needed to get them excited, and out of their seats a little bit, and that's something I tried to do."

Anthony Carter did plenty of that. For all of us who watched his exploits, and marveled at his abilities, there are memories galore. He was one of a kind. He was "A. C."

"What Was That?"

Back in 1991, Michigan's second player to ever win the coveted Heisman Trophy started his run for the Heisman early in the year. After a great game against Boston College on the road, Desmond Howard returned to Ann Arbor with his Michigan teammates to face Notre Dame.

The hype for the game was immense. The Wolverines were ranked No. 3 in the country, and Notre Dame was ranked No. 7. It was a nationally televised affair. All eyes of the college football world were on Ann Arbor that Saturday, and Desmond made the most of it.

It was a tight game throughout, but late in the contest with Michigan holding a slim three-point lead, fate and a mistake stepped in and started a historic season for Desmond Howard.

It was fourth down. Michigan was close enough for a field-goal attempt, but head coach Gary Moeller was rolling the dice—or was he? As Elvis Grbac, the Wolverine quarterback, came to the line to

The catch that broke Notre Dame.

call signals, there were some who thought Michigan was just trying to pull the Irish offsides. Then the ball was snapped, and all bets were off.

Desmond Howard was right in the middle of it. "Actually, Elvis checked into that play," Howard says, "but we weren't sure we were going to stick with it because they rolled the coverage to 'cover two.' I came off the ball hard, and I looked, and I saw Elvis cock it to throw it, so I knew he was going to stick with the play. I ran as hard as I could, as fast as I could, and I thought the ball was still overthrown. I finally stretched as far as I could, and I was blessed with a heck of a diving catch."

The play sent Michigan Stadium into a frenzy, but Coach Moeller wasn't so thrilled while the ball was in the air. "Mo" wasn't exactly on the same page as Desmond and Elvis, "[Coach Moeller] probably was wondering, '*What was that?*'" Desmond says. "But everyone was so happy and so excited because that was the first time we had beaten Notre Dame in so long, nobody placed a lot of emphasis on the checkoff at the line of scrimmage. They were just really excited about the win. It was a little bit of confusion that ended up well."

It ended up well indeed, for Michigan and Desmond. Howard knew that after that game and his special play, he was going to be in the running for the Heisman. "When you have a big game against a team like Notre Dame on national television, " Howard says today, "people are going to stand up and take notice of your talents."

They took enough notice that Desmond won the Heisman Trophy after the 1991 season in a landslide vote.

"We Don't Make That Decision!"

It is clear to all of us that the events of September 11, 2001, have changed our world. Sporting events in this country were cancelled or postponed the weekend following the terrorist attacks in New York and Washington. The Michigan football game with Western Michigan was one of those postponed events, but you might be surprised to know that in previous years, Michigan Stadium has seen turmoil that threatened scheduled events.

During the Vietnam War, Don Canham ruled the athletic department at Michigan. Those who lived through those years on a college campus like the University of Michigan know just how turbulent they were. Canham was one of those who had to deal with trouble quickly and responsibly. "The terrorist attack in September reminds me so much of the Vietnam era," Canham recalls. "Every day, I mean every day, we'd get a phone call from some nut telling us they were going to put a bomb in the Stadium."

With 100,000 guests expected in the Stadium for a home football game, Canham took every one of these calls seriously, and made sure Michigan had a plan to ensure everyone's safety.

Canham set up an operation to make sure the Stadium would be secure. "Don Lund, our assistant athletic director," Canham recalls, "put a crew together. On Thursday before a game, they would start sweeping the stadium, checking all the restrooms, all the concession stands. We did it right up until game time. So we knew there were no bombs in the Stadium."

Canham recalls today, though, that the anxiety for some others in the security community wasn't over. "We'd go to the Stadium on game day and we'd get a phone call in the press box. It was the FBI. They weren't aware that we had been sweeping the Stadium for three days," Canham now remembers with a chuckle. "They would then come to me and say, all excited, 'This looks like a serious threat.' I would then ask them what they thought I should do, and they would tell me, 'Oh, we don't make that decision, that's up to you.' So, here I am in the press box with my family, and the FBI says I've got a serious threat. We knew we had taken care of it because we'd thoroughly swept the place.

"You know," Canham continued, "some stadiums, at that time, actually cleared the stadium. Lots of baseball parks did that, but we swept Michigan Stadium completely. We had a great chief of police in Ann Arbor and a great sheriff who both helped us tremendously, so we knew it was clean."

"I Never Got Fired During a Game"

One of the great reasons for the incredible success of Bo Schembechler in his career at Michigan was that he hired outstanding assistant coaches. Throughout the years, a number of his assistants have gone on to head coaching jobs and done extremely well. One of the best that Bo brought with him from Miami of Ohio was Jerry Hanlon. Hanlon stayed with Bo at Michigan until Bo retired, and then he continued with the Wolverines into Gary Moeller's tenure as coach before Jerry finally retired.

Jerry and Bo have a great relationship. Bo has nicknamed Hanlon "Rocko." I'm not sure why, but it seems to fit. While Jerry is short in stature, or should I say, not very tall, there isn't a man alive who loves Michigan as much. There also isn't a man alive who knows as much about football or has as much passion for the game or can strike the fear of the Lord into young men twice his size when they don't perform to their capabilities. He was my position coach when I played at Michigan, and if you haven't figured it out by now, I like him a lot.

Hanlon has a great football mind, and he was a perfect fit to be on Schembechler's staff. Jerry wasn't a guy who would back down from Bo. If there was an argument on how to block a play or what play to run in a given situation, Jerry gave as good as he got, and Bo could dish it out pretty well.

The difficulty with the situation was that Bo was the head coach, and whenever Jerry kept after him or frustrated him enough, Bo would stand up and say, "Hanlon, you're fired!" It was Bo's trump card. He not only did it once; he did it a hundred times.

If they weren't such good friends or didn't respect the other's abilities so much, they couldn't have coexisted. Their relationship is still strong today, and Hanlon still gets a chuckle out of the days when he and Bo were battling each other in the common cause of Wolverine victories. "I never got fired during a game," Hanlon laughs. "I do remember that I was threatened to be fired during a game, but he never went through with it. Normally the firings came in meetings when we would disagree on certain things that were going to take place.

"Somebody asked me one time, what was the secret of coaching with Schembechler? I told them it was to get hired one more time than you got fired! That was my basic philosophy."

Michigan football is lucky Hanlon had that philosophy. Over his years at Michigan, he helped create a program that became nationally renowned for developing great offensive line talent. Hanlon was considered one of the finest offensive line coaches in the country during his tenure at Michigan. When he was moved to the backfield and took on the duties of quarterbacks coach, he did just as well, developing the likes of All-American Jim Harbaugh.

All this from a guy Bo fired on a regular basis!

Hanlon coaches one of his troops at practice.

The Worst Thing He Ever Said

Jerry Hanlon and Bo Schembechler have been through a lot in their days at Michigan, and Hanlon is a great source of information regarding Bo's legendary volcanic personality. This story is about one of those eruptions. Surprisingly, according to Hanlon, this outburst contained no four-letter words. It wasn't uttered above a normal speaking voice, yet Jerry tells me that it was the worst thing he ever heard Bo say to a referee.

"The truth of the matter," Hanlon says, "Bo very seldom hollered at officials. He would talk to them when an official walked close to the bench. That was when he would get on officials. To holler out at them on the field, I don't remember him doing a lot of that. It was when they got close to the sideline is when he would let them know what he felt about certain things in no uncertain terms.

"The best one, though," Jerry continued with a smile, "wasn't in our Stadium. We were on the road at Wisconsin one year and we were walking off the field after the game. Bo was so mad at one of the officials. You've got to understand, the officiating was bad. We were all mad. Anyway, we were walking off the field and this official was walking in front of us. Bo said, *'You walk like a girl!'*"
Hanlon laughs out loud at the memory of that one. "I thought that was the worst thing he could have said, but that was his comment. It was the biggest put-down I may have ever heard from him to an official."

"Run the Damn Ball over Me!"

There have been hundreds of great performances at Michigan Stadium. Most of them involve running backs, quarterbacks, receivers, defensive linemen, or linebackers. If you've attended games at The Big House for any length of time, I'm sure you have your own favorite game by a player. Rarely, though, do you hear about a defining moment for an offensive lineman. Jerry Hanlon remembers one of those moments. It was a performance by one of the best offensive linemen to ever wear the Maize and Blue. It came from Dan Dierdorf in his senior season.

Dan came to Ann Arbor from Canton, Ohio. He had actually been recruited by Bo Schembechler to go to Miami of Ohio, but he turned Bo down. He also turned Woody Hayes down when the Buckeye coach tried to get him to Ohio State.

Dan chose Michigan instead, thanks to a great recruiting job by Bump Elliott. Dan started as a sophomore for the Wolverines and got better every year after that. In his senior season, he was a consensus All-American, and after leaving the Wolverine program, he went on to an NFL Hall of Fame career with the St. Louis Cardinals.

The testament to Dan's abilities came in the third game of his senior year when Michigan was battling Texas A&M in Ann Arbor. Coach Hanlon was the offensive line coach, and he still marvels at what happened that afternoon. "Texas A&M had come off their opener at Ohio State where they just got hammered. They got caught in a buzz saw down there in an opening game," Hanlon remembers. "They then stayed in the Midwest for a week of practice instead of flying back to Texas. After seeing their loss to Ohio State, we took the field that day thinking that it might be an easy game, but they had some good football players. They had a real strong team. They just didn't play well in Ohio."

Jerry remembers that it was anything but an easy game for Michigan. "We just struggled and struggled," Hanlon says, "and we were down, I think 10-7, going into the fourth quarter. I remember Dierdorf coming off the field to the sideline, and he got on the phone to me in the press box. He said, 'What's wrong, Coach? Why aren't we moving the ball?'

"I said, 'I'll tell you what's wrong. We won't knock anybody off the line of scrimmage.'" Hanlon remembers Dan's response like it was yesterday. "I saw him look up at me in the press box from the field. He was looking right at me when I heard him over the phone say, *'Run the damn ball over me!'*

"The next time we got the ball," Hanlon recalls, "it was at the 20-yard line. We ran 26 and 27, which was an off-tackle play over our strong tackle. We'd go Red 26, which was to the right, and White 27, which was to the left. At that time, we flipped our strong tackle to both sides based on the formation. We ran that ball behind Dierdorf every darn play. We took it right straight down the field. Now don't get me wrong, the other guys were blocking, too, but Dierdorf was at the point of attack. We ran it right down the field to the two-yard line. At that point, Bo called a 28, which was a quarterback keeper around the right end.

"When Bo called that play," Hanlon says with a chuckle, "I darn near quit my job right then and there. I wanted to take it all the way in behind Dan. Of course we scored on the 28. By the time we faked off-tackle, every defender was inside; [Don] Moorhead walked into the end zone.

Opponents never escaped when Dan Dierdorf flew at them.

"It really was a defining moment for Dan and for the team. We were down. It looked like we were going to lose," Hanlon continues, "and somebody took it on their shoulders and showed everybody how it was done."

Michigan went on to win that game 14-10. We won every game that year until the finale at Ohio State. The closest Wolverine margin of victory the rest of the season was 14 points.

The Secret Shoes

The rivalry between Michigan and Ohio State has spawned lots of stories. This one comes from equipment manager Jon Falk. It really points out the kind of attention both teams focused on each other throughout the season. Buckeye head coach Woody Hayes was legendary in his obsession with keeping Michigan on his radar screen, and this tale from Michigan Stadium is a perfect example.

It was in the mid- to late 1970s, according to Falk. "We were playing on that Tartan artificial surface," Jon says, "and when it rained it was really slick. It was like playing on ice. I remember Ara Parseghian calling Bo and telling him about some football shoes that were made over in Canada. The shoes were supposed to be great on a wet artificial surface. So Bo told me to get some, and I ordered a few pair to check them out.

"The last scrimmage before the season, fortunately for us, it rained," Jon says. "Well, I put those shoes on a few guys, and after practice the kids told me that the new shoes were a lot better than the ones we had been wearing. We ordered 150 pairs of those shoes the very next day. We flew them in from Canada and had them here. We only used them when it rained. They were way too grippy when it was dry.

"All season," Falk remembers with delight, "I'll be darned if it didn't rain almost every home game. Teams were coming in and slipping all over the place, while we were standing in there with good footing. Even the Minnesota equipment guy called me Sunday morning after we beat them 45-0. He asked me where we got the shoes. He said his job might be on the line if he didn't find out about our shoes.

"I can remember walking into the locker room on rainy Saturdays," Jon says, "and I'd yell, 'OK guys, it's a Tiger Paw day. It's time to get those Tiger Paws on.'"

All was going along well with Jon and the shoes until the week before the Ohio State game. Apparently, the Wolverines' footing on wet days was under consideration in Columbus. "An article came out in the *Columbus Dispatch*," Falk says. "Woody Hayes was quoted as saying that Michigan had secret shoes! Woody said, in the article, that he had been studying the films, and he found out about these secret shoes that Michigan wore to play on the wet field. Woody went out and got the shoes for his team for the game against us."

Jon says the suspicion about the shoes was an issue right up until game time. "The day before the game, Ohio State came in to work out," Jon recalls. "I had left our locker room door open. I came walking up the tunnel, and I saw some Ohio State players sneaking across the way into our locker room. They were looking at our shoes! I heard them as they came out, and they were saying, 'Yeah, they're the same shoes.'"

As it turned out, the shoes didn't help the Buckeyes. Falk remembers Michigan winning the game 14-6 the following day. But Jon says he'll never forget the attention to detail by Coach Hayes. He studied the film and made some phone calls. He identified the shoes and got some for his team. He had put his squad on equal footing, so to speak. It's no wonder why Woody won so much at Ohio State. He didn't miss a trick.

They Were Ready to Get Ripped

Another coach who never missed a trick was Woody's protégé, and his nemesis on occasion, Bo Schembechler. Bo readily admits he learned a great deal from Woody. He put a lot of what he learned to work when he was coaching Michigan. When it came to psychology and motivation, Bo was a master. He may have learned some of the basics from Woody, but Bo took the art a step further in his days as the Wolverines' head coach. He may not have had a degree in psychology, but when he needed to, he instinctively knew what actions were necessary to rally the troops.

One such instance occurred in 1988. The Wolverines had opened the season with two straight losses. Notre Dame had beaten Michigan 19-17 in South Bend in their opener, and the following week, in Ann Arbor, Miami of Florida came away with a 31-30 win. Both games were heartbreaking losses. The Irish won in the last two minutes of a tight game. The Hurricanes overcame a big Michigan lead to win in the final minute. Everybody expected Schembechler to be at his surly best following the Miami loss in the postgame press interview. An 0-2 start was not acceptable, and most of the press and players thought Bo would read everybody the riot act.

In a stroke of genius, Bo surprised everybody, "In the press conference after the Miami loss," Bo says, "I just told the press that they had just seen the Big Ten champions play. I told them that we were going to win the conference championship. I felt very strongly about that. You've got to understand, Miami and Notre Dame were two great teams, and we could have beaten both of them. We didn't do it, but we could have. I just felt that we would get our team together and win the championship."

It was not the message most had expected at that time. The media reported Bo's comments accurately in the Sunday papers, but to be honest, there was a sense that Bo was putting a good spin on a bad situation. Nothing could have been further from the truth. Bo knew exactly what he was doing in that press conference. He was sending a message to his team through the media.

"I'm sure it had an effect on them. All of them were ready to get ripped!" Bo laughs. "And all of a sudden, here I am, saying we are going to win the Big Ten championship. I think that helped."

To say it helped was an understatement. The Wolverines *did* go on to win the conference title. They didn't lose another game the rest of the year. The only blemish on their record was a tie at Iowa. After wrapping up the title with a 34-31 win at Ohio State, the Wolverines went on to beat Southern Cal 22-14 in the Rose Bowl.

Michigan finished the year ranked fourth in the national standings. Notre Dame and Miami, the only teams to beat Michigan, were ranked first and second. Florida State finished third.

It turned out to be a great year for a team that started 0-2, and much of that success can be traced back to that press conference in Michigan Stadium when Coach Schembechler surprised the media and revitalized his team.

He Called the Finish!

Michigan and Iowa have had some great finishes over the years, but two games in successive seasons stand out. In 1985, the Wolverines and Hawkeyes met in Iowa City. Iowa was ranked No. 1 in the nation, and Michigan was ranked No. 2. It was a highly anticipated game, and it proved to be everything it was billed to be. The game was decided in the final seconds. Iowa's Rob Houghtlin kicked a field goal with two seconds left, and Iowa came away with a 12-10 win.

The following year, back in Ann Arbor at Michigan Stadium, the two teams met again. This time, Michigan was ranked fourth in the country, and Iowa entered the game ranked eighth. Once again, it came down to the final seconds. This time, though, Mike Gillette kicked a field goal for Michigan with no time left, and the Wolverines were victorious 20-17.

Both games were great theater. Both games featured amazing plays. Both games featured amazing finishes. What may have been most amazing, though, is that Michigan defensive coordinator at the time, Gary Moeller, predicted the finish of the 1986 game before kickoff.

It is a tale from Michigan Stadium that Erik Campbell will never forget. Erik, who was a defensive back on those teams, played in both games. "Moeller told us in a meeting that he actually visualized the game," Erik remembers. "He said it was going to come down to the very end. I had an interception right before the half. The game then came down to the Gillette field goal, just like 'Mo' had described it. He even told us the stands would empty out, just like they had the previous year in Iowa City. So, when Gillette made the field goal, the stands emptied out, just like he said, and we had fans all over the field."

Campbell still remembers how amazed he was as it all unfolded before him. "He called it!" Erik exclaimed of Moeller's premonition. "He said we were going to make a last-second play, the fans were going to storm the field, and it happened just like he described it. It was unbelievable. He had this vision, and it came out true."

"I've Got Good News and Bad News"

Football is a tough, physical game. The players are big, fast, and strong. It's hard to get through a season without some injuries because of the physical nature of the game. Players are in the midst of the battle all the time, but you rarely hear about the coaches who sometimes get a little too close to the action.

This story comes from Bobby Morrison, the former special teams coach for the Wolverines. It was in the national championship season of 1997, and it all started at a practice when Morrison was in the wrong spot at the wrong time. "We were at practice one day," Morrison says, "and we had just finished stretching. I was standing right by a group of the big guys. When we broke from the stretching and ran to our next drill, I was in the way of Jon Jansen."

Jon Jansen was an offensive tackle. He was about six foot six and just over 300 pounds. He was a team captain and leader, so he always ran to the next drill. "When Jansen turned and sprinted to the next drill," Morrison recalls painfully, "I was right in his way. Needless to say, he caught me right in the chest, knocked the wind out of me, and I thought I was close to death! I recovered, though, and coached the rest of that day, and I was alright."

The story continues a couple of weeks later, when Michigan was playing Wisconsin. Sometime during the game, Michigan forced a Wisconsin punt, and Morrison, as the special teams coach, was concentrating hard on the play. "We had put two guys on their wide coverage guy, their 'gunner,' we called him," Morrison says with a laugh. "So we are jamming the gunner, and I'm watching the flight of the ball. I'm kind of backing up on the sidelines watching the ball. I'm moving down the field, and we are kicking the hell out of their gunner. Our guys have blocked him out of bounds on our sideline, but he's still running. Well, he hits me, and all I remember were the doctors. They were the first to get to me. They carry me back to the bench. As soon as the game was over, they took me over to emergency at the hospital."

Bobby said he was hurting from the collision and had some concerns while waiting for the X-rays. "Finally the doctor came out," Bobby recalls, "and he says, 'I've got good news and bad news.' So I said give me the good news first, and he says, 'The good news is that you did not break any ribs today.' I said, 'Well, what's the bad news?' He said, 'When Jansen hit you two weeks ago, you broke two ribs.'"

Bobby never made the injury report, but he'd been coaching two weeks with broken ribs from his own player.

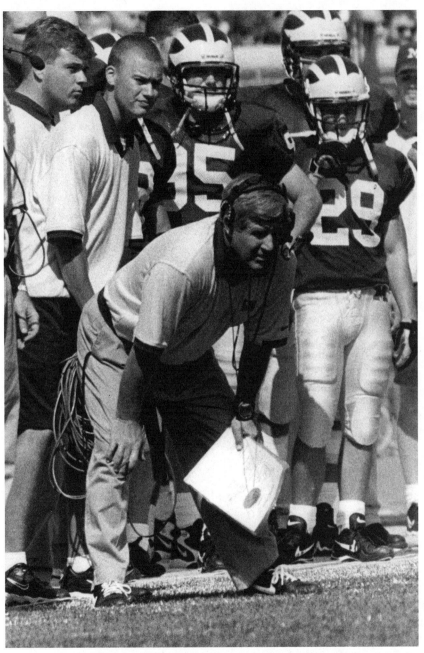

Morrison keeps his eye on the "gunner."

"Tell Fred He's on Fire!"

Sometimes you concentrate so much when you're in the middle of a game, you lose track of things and situations around you. It can happen to a player. It can happen to a coach. This next story happened in Wisconsin during a cold November game in 1997.

We start with the observations of Stan Parrish who, at the time, was the quarterbacks coach. He was on the sidelines working with his quarterbacks during this bitterly cold day. "We were ranked No. 1 in the country by this time," says Parrish, "and we were getting the ball back from Wisconsin. Remember, it was really freezing there, and Fred Jackson, our running backs coach, was down at the same end of the bench as I was, and we were working with the kids. I was getting ready to give [Brian] Griese the opening play for the possession when I heard someone say in my headset that Fred was on fire!

"Now there is always a little bit of levity in football," Parrish continues, "but it was exactly the case. I turn and see that Fred's gloves are on fire and singeing. In all the tension of the day and the moment, those are the kinds of things you remember forever."

For Fred Jackson, it wasn't so funny at the time. The explanation of this event is understandable, if not incredible. "I don't know the exact temperature up there in Wisconsin," Jackson remembers, "but it was cold as it could be at a football game. I was talking with our running backs, Chris Howard and Chris Floyd, who had just come out of the game and they were sitting on the bench right next to one of those big long burners. You know, the kind they use to keep the players warm. You can see fire coming out of the very end of those things."

At this point, Jackson made the mistake of underestimating the heat generated by the burner. "While I was talking to the kids," Fred says with an embarrassed chuckle, "telling them what we were going to do on the next series, I put my hands down in front of the burner and rubbed them together to warm them up. I turned back around and Chris Floyd said, 'Coach, your gloves are on fire!' I looked at my hands, and the tips of my gloves were burning. I could

Fred Jackson in a less heated environment.

see I didn't have time to take the gloves off, so I stuck my hands in front of Floyd and Howard, and they slapped the fire out.

"The fire hadn't started to burn my fingers," laughs Jackson. "So I wasn't hurt or anything, but wouldn't you know, Stan Parrish saw it. The next thing I hear in my headset is, 'Damn, Fred's on fire!'"

Michigan went on to beat Wisconsin that day in a tough road game. They would finish the year unbeaten and win a national title. But one of the most memorable flights home from a road trip that year was coming back from Wisconsin. There was more talk about Fred catching on fire than there was about the game.

It Was Double-Bad

There are times during a game when you are sure something will work against an opponent. So you go with it, and it blows up in your face. Nobody feels worse than the guy who decided to go with the play. Such is the case of Michigan quarterback Dick Vidmer in the 1966 season against Illinois.

Vidmer was the signal caller in the 1966 season, and a darned good one. As a matter of fact, you might consider him one of the least recognized of the starting quarterbacks because of the success Michigan has had since 1980. For example, Vidmer had the most prolific passing yardage season of any Michigan quarterback before 1981. He threw for more yards than both Wangler and Leach in a single season. In one game against Oregon State in September 1966, Vidmer was 12 of 18 through the air for 258 yards. That averages to over 21 yards per completion. Vidmer will tell you, though, that he might give up all those numbers to have that one pass back against Illinois in The Big House.

"Oh, my God," Dick moaned when I reminded him of the play. "We threw it to the wide side of the field, the ball was tipped, an Illinois defensive back got it and raced down the field 99 yards for a touchdown. That was the worst moment of my college football career. I would just as soon forget that, but I can't! I guess the good comes with the bad," Vidmer now says philosophically.

What made the interception even worse for Dick and the Wolverines is that coach Bump Elliot had told him not to throw the ball. "He did say *not* to throw it, but we thought in the huddle," remembers Vidmer, "that we had a better chance of success to the wide side of the field. Of course, it was a big mistake at the time. Sometimes you try your own and it doesn't work. That's when it's double-bad, I mean, *double-bad*."

Double-bad indeed. Michigan lost the game to Illinois that day, 28-21. The interception came with less than eight minutes to play. Michigan would finish the season at 6-4 that year, and Vidmer had a prolific season. He just wishes he had that one pass back.

According to Dick Vidmer, "The good comes with the bad."

He Was a Very Gentle Guy

One of the greatest names in Michigan football history is Bennie Oosterbaan. Not only was he one of the best football players ever at Michigan, but he also was a great Wolverine coach. He coached the 1948 squad that won a national title. His Wolverines outscored their opponents 252-44 during that season. Bennie's name is mentioned right along with Yost and Crisler when a discussion turns to the Michigan tradition. One of the players who had a special relationship with Bennie is the legendary Wolverine end, Ron Kramer.

"He was the most nostalgic guy," recalls Kramer, "and a wonderful motivator as a speaker. He was a traditionalist. I mean, he *was* Michigan tradition. I had such great love for him, and he never, ever lost his cool. He never yelled and screamed at anybody.

"At practice most of the time, you'd see him sitting over on the bench. It was as if he were saying, 'I'm the head coach. I'll let my assistant coaches coach. I'm going to motivate.'"

Ron also says that Oosterbaan wasn't just a figurehead, however. He could also coach. "He did have some good innovations," Kramer continues, "off the Wing-T and the Single-Wing formation. That's what we played when I was in school. We had to play offense and defense. Bennie was always the kind of guy that was very kind. He was a very gentle sort to the day he died."

Despite his laid-back nature, Bennie was a guy who could get the best out of his talent. There was no lack of intensity on his teams, according to Kramer. "You know how intense we got at the University of Michigan?" Ron asked. "We had guys on my team that were between 165 and 180 pounds playing offensive and defensive guard! Now, how would you like to be those guys playing against Alex Karras and players like that? These guys held their own against them. That, to me, is intensity! The motivator was Bennie Oosterbaan himself. Bennie was that kind of guy."

Gentle Ben Oosterbaan.

Where Is Bennie?

Ron Kramer and Bennie Oosterbaan had a very special relationship. Well after he graduated and went on to stardom in the National Football League, Kramer remained very close to his former head coach. As a matter of fact, Ron tells a story that is as touching as you'll find.

Kramer starts with the history of his relationship with Bennie. "Whenever I went to Ann Arbor," Ron said nostalgically, "I always stopped to see him. Bennie kind of adopted me, not formally, but he considered me like a son. I was similar to what he was at the University of Michigan. He was a three-sport man, a three-letter man, football, basketball, and baseball. I was the same, except that I ran track instead of playing baseball. So, he just sort of adopted ol' Krames.

"And I felt the same way about him," Kramer says. "I used to bring my new girlfriends over to see him! I used to bring my dogs over to meet him! He loved my dogs. We used to take little walks, because in his later years he needed to get some exercise. We'd walk down this little pathway in his backyard. Occasionally, we'd sit and watch a little TV. He would always give me a few words of wisdom. He would tell me how well he thought current coaches were doing. He would tell me how wonderful the University of Michigan was, and how glad he was that he was considered such a big part of the Michigan tradition.

"Then Bennie got sick, not long after his wife died," recalls Kramer, "and they took him over to one of those homes. One Wednesday, when I went to visit him, he said, 'Ron, I'm not going to make it.' I said, 'Bennie, you'll be fine.' And I left and went home. I got a call the next morning that Bennie had died in his sleep that night. We had his funeral. We eulogized him. Bo Schembechler eulogized him, too, because Bo really liked Bennie a lot."

It was a sad time because Ron and Bennie were so close, but there was one more gesture Ron performed for his old coach and friend.

Ron Kramer and Bennie Oosterbaan together, friends for life.

"About four days after Bennie had passed, I get a call from the funeral parlor," remembers Kramer. "They tell me that they've got Bennie's remains, and they don't know what to do with the ashes."

Ron told the funeral home he didn't know what to do with the remains, but the funeral parlor director persisted, "Nobody has called, nobody has taken charge. You've got to do something about this," Kramer remembers him saying. "I said, OK, fine. So I went over and picked up Bennie's remains." Ron recalls. "Bennie's remains were in this box. It had a label on it that read 'Remains of Bennie Oosterbaan.'" Kramer chuckles about it today, but there he was with Bennie under his arm.

"I looked at the box," Kramer remembers with a smile, "and I said, 'Well Bennie, I think I'm going to take you out. You haven't been out for a long time.' So I'd go to a bar, and I'd put him on the bar. I'd have a drink, and Bennie used to drink bourbon and water, so I'd order bourbon and water for him. The bartenders at these places would ask me who the drink was for, and I'd say it was for Bennie. 'He's not with us anymore, he's in the box.' Most of the bartenders were guys I knew at these local pubs, so they'd look at me and tell me I was a real nut, which I was!

"After a while," said Ron, "I really didn't know what to do with Bennie. So, I quietly went over to visit his house one day and ponder the relationship that I had with him, you know, the great love I had for him and the love he had for me. I took some of the remains with me and I walked down the little pathway he and I used to walk when I visited, and I spread some of his remains there. As I thought about this, I said to myself, 'I think I'll go over to Ferry Field.' Michigan had played at Ferry Field before they opened Michigan Stadium, and I spread some of his remains there."

Ron says he continued on this journey of respect with Bennie's ashes to the entire athletic complex. "I went over to the baseball diamond, and I walked around the base paths and spread some of his ashes. I did the same at Yost Field House. I went over to the Bennie Oosterbaan indoor practice facility and spread some over there."

Kramer then remembered another spot that would hold a special place in Bennie's memory. "When I was in school, we would stay at the golf course on Friday nights and walk over to the Stadium on game days. We'd walk across Stadium Boulevard, down the tunnel, on to the field, and back up the tunnel to the locker room and dress for the game. So I took Bennie to the golf course, and walked along the same route. I walked down the tunnel and around the field spreading a little of his ashes here and there. By the time I got to the top of the tunnel, Bennie was gone.

"To me, that is my great tribute to a man I absolutely adored." Ron says with reverence. "He was *wonderful,* and he *deserves* to be everywhere Bennie is now."

I have often referred to Michigan Stadium as hallowed ground. When Ron related this story to me, I realized the Stadium really is hallowed ground. When they talk about the ghosts of Crisler, Yost, and Oosterbaan roaming around the Stadium at night, I tend to believe it now.

Not surprisingly, there were some people who told me after they had heard Ron's story that it wouldn't be such a bad idea to have their ashes scattered around the Stadium when their time came!

"If You're Going to Fight in the North Atlantic..."

Those who played for Bo Schembechler have a wealth of tales to tell about Bo. Whenever we have reunions, we always have a great time telling each other what we affectionately call "Bo stories." Schembechler claims that we embellish these tales way too much. He swears he didn't do half the things we say he did. While he may be correct in some instances, there are others that he knows are true, and this is one of them.

In Bo's first year at Michigan, we were preparing for a game late in the season. During the week of the game we had a terrible snowstorm in Ann Arbor, and everything was covered in snow, including our practice field. All day long, the players had wondered where we would practice that day. Back then, there was no indoor practice facility with artificial turf. The only place we had to practice indoors was Yost Field House. The prospect of practicing in Yost on the hard dirt surface and cinders was not very pleasant. We were all kind of curious what Bo would do that day, considering Mother Nature's assault on his practice schedule.

When we got to Yost in the afternoon to dress and get ready for practice, we heard rumors that the assistant coaches, managers, and some freshmen had been out on the practice field shoveling snow. We couldn't imagine that Bo was really considering going outside, but we weren't sure. We had seen him do some things we hadn't seen done before, so we all got ready as if it were a normal day. In the back of our minds, though, we thought indoors would be the choice.

As we all started our march down the stairs to the door leading from Yost to the outside and practice, we were told to wait. At that point, we figured Bo had made his decision, and we would be practicing indoors. We gathered around in groups. Some stretched; some just stood talking. We were waiting for Bo to appear. He hadn't been around from the time we had arrived to dress for practice.

Finally, the small door to Yost flew open, and Bo strode in wearing his Michigan hat and a heavy coat. Snow was sticking to him. He yelled, "Bring it up, men!"

We gathered in a big circle around him. He said, "It's pretty rough weather out there. But remember what Admiral King said to his troops in World War II: 'If you're going to *fight* in the North Atlantic, you've got to *train* in the North Atlantic!' *Ok, now let's go!*"

With that, Bo turned and ran to the door and into the elements outside. We all roared and followed him into the wind and snow. None of us knew who Admiral King was, and we had no clue whether Admiral King had ever said such a thing, but we practiced two hours outside on a field that had been shoveled semi-clean.

The following Saturday, we played on the road in cold conditions. As I recall, there wasn't a lot of snow, maybe a few flurries during the game, but we won handily. We never questioned again whether we would practice indoors or outdoors. Bo had made his point. If he was going to take his team to play in the snow, he was certainly going to make his team practice in it, too.

Thank you, Admiral King!

Clarence "Biggie" Munn

When you see the name "Biggie" Munn heading up a story in a book that is relating tales from Michigan Stadium, you're probably wondering how in the world his name got in the mix. It's really very simple. Clarence "Biggie" Munn was an assistant coach at Michigan for eight years, from 1938 to 1945. Munn worked as an assistant coach for Fritz Crisler during his years in Ann Arbor.

Of course, Munn's career took on legendary proportions when he moved up the road to Michigan State and took over as the head football coach. He also served as the Spartans' athletic director and today is considered one of the founding fathers of athletics in East Lansing.

It was during his years with Crisler, though, that Munn learned his trade, and he learned it very well. One of the players who remembers "Biggie" when he was wearing Maize and Blue is Hercules Renda. Renda played for the Wolverines in 1937, 1938, and 1939. He was a halfback who hailed from Jochin, West Virginia, a town Hercules admits, "doesn't exist anymore." In the early going of the relationship between Crisler and Munn, though, Renda was an eyewitness to the clash of wills between the two titans.

One particular story that Renda tells about Crisler and his attention to discipline on his team and his staff revolves around Munn. "Biggie told me to never tell anybody this," Hercules told me in a conspiratorial tone. "But, since he's passed, I guess it will be OK," Renda continued. "One day, Coach Crisler had sent Biggie on an errand in the morning, and he didn't get it done on time and was late for practice.

"Crisler had a thing about practice. When you got dressed in your uniform for practice and got to the field, you always had to

Photo courtesy of Bentley Historical Library, University of Michigan

"Biggie" Munn (fourth from right) as a Wolverine coach,
next to Fritz Crisler (third from right).

run down to the wall at the end of Ferry Field and run back to your position," Renda recalls. "Now, Munn arrived late to practice after running the errand. When he showed up, Crisler made him run to the wall and back! *Biggie was an assistant coach!* Crisler had made him run to the wall. Munn told me in later years that he was never so mad at anybody in his life than he was that day with Crisler," Renda recalls with a chuckle.

"More than anything, though," Hercules went on, "that incident tells you something about Crisler as a coach."

Hercules was also impressed with Munn. Munn was Michigan's line coach during Renda's career at Michigan, and Renda says Munn developed some great players, but it was an incident many years later that Hercules says was the real measure of Biggie Munn. "Michigan is playing Michigan State," Renda recalls, "and it's years later, when Biggie is the athletic director of Michigan State. State is playing in Ann Arbor. Before the game, I'm walking down the aisle to my seat, and on the way down, I see Biggie coming up that same aisle. So I thought I'd say hi to the coach before I sat down. When we got near one another, I reached out to shake his hand and said, 'Hi, Coach.'"

Renda recalls that Munn looked at him quizzically at first and then said, "Don't tell me." For a moment, he just looked at him. Then he said, "No. 85."

And I thought, *"Wow!"* Think of the years that had passed when he was the line coach at Michigan, and all of the kids he had been involved with, at Syracuse, then at Michigan State, and then as athletic director. For a man to remember my number! It was amazing!"

"I Didn't Know What the Hell He Was Doing!"

In 1997, Michigan won the national championship by completing their season undefeated, which included a win in the Rose Bowl over Washington State. I can tell you that in a season like that, there are a lot of memories. Every player has his own special moment or two that he'll never forget. Some of those moments aren't about plays. It's an interesting exercise, finding out from players and coaches what made their list of great moments during that season.

James Hall played defensive end for the Wolverines in 1997, and he begins his list with a scary moment from the third game that season against Notre Dame. "The first series, they took it like 12 plays," remembers Hall. "We were out there, and we were tired, and we thought it was going to be a long day. They got it down close to score, and it came down to a fourth-down play. We stopped them. That was a great feeling right there."

From that scare, Michigan went on to beat Notre Dame 21-14. Previously, the Wolverines had beaten Colorado and Baylor, which got them headed into the Big Ten season with a 3-0 non-conference start.

The next moment that stands out for Hall came on the road. In game seven, against Michigan State, the Wolverines won a 23-7 decision, but a play by Charles Woodson stunned Hall and everybody else who was watching that day.

The Spartans were attempting to throw, but Michigan had everybody covered. The Michigan State quarterback decided to throw the ball away rather than take a sack. He threw the ball toward the sideline. It appeared to be well overthrown until Woodson rose up out of a mass of players near the sideline. He stretched his arm straight up over his head as far as possible and pulled the ball down with one hand. At the same time, he twisted his body awkwardly while in the air, so that when he came down, he landed with one foot in bounds for an interception. The entire stadium gasped. Nobody could believe that Woodson did what they all just saw, including Hall.

"I was on the field for that play," Hall recalls, "and I didn't know what the hell he was doing when he jumped up. I don't even know why he jumped, because the ball was clearly going out of bounds. I thought to myself, 'He's not about to do this.' And when he went up there and got that ball, I stopped and said, 'Dang!'" Hall laughs today at his own reaction and added with a teammate's humor, "He did that for show, all the way!"

Woodson would win the Heisman Trophy that year. The interception against State was just one of the many brilliant plays he made. Hall says Charles really pulled the rest of the team along with him that year. "He made some really impressive plays that year. He took it to another level. He was a big part of our team success."

When Michigan closed that year out with a win over Ohio State to finish unbeaten and maintain their No. 1 national ranking, they did it at Michigan Stadium. Woodson was again outstanding, intercepting a key pass and returning a punt for a touchdown. While that is a lasting memory for Hall, it is what happened immediately after the game that stands out. "After we won and went up the tunnel to the locker room, we saw the roses in our lockers," Hall says. "That's all you hear about, is getting that rose in the locker once you're going to the Rose Bowl. Then we came back down the tunnel and out into the stadium. The whole Stadium is filled with people, running all over the field. We were just out there celebrating with our peers, students, and fans, enjoying the moment. We had the

Big Ten championship trophy presentation on the field, and we put Eric Mayes, one of our captains, on our shoulders and carried him off the field. Wow," Hall sighs, "that was one of the best memories in The Big House for me."

It was for a lot of Michigan fans, James.

"I Was More Relieved Than Anything..."

The 1997 season produced a pair of magical moments for assistant coach Stan Parrish. At the time, Parrish was the quarterbacks coach for the Wolverines. It was during their battles against Iowa and Ohio State, both at Michigan Stadium, that Parrish says there were defining moments for him.

In the Iowa game, the entire unbeaten season was beginning to look shaky. The Hawkeyes had built up a lead over Michigan. Just before the half, Iowa's great receiver and return man, Tim Dwight, had shocked everybody in the Stadium with a punt return for a score, and the Wolverines were forced into a come-back position in the second half. The problem with a second-half comeback was that the Wolverines had played maybe their poorest half of football ever to that point. It would be a tall order to rescue victory against the fired-up Hawkeyes.

Michigan did fight back in that game, and in the fourth quarter, they started a drive from their own territory to win it. Trailing 24-21, Parrish was on the sidelines keeping quarterback Brian Griese on track to pull it out. "Brian, you know, had thrown three interceptions in the first half," Parrish laments, "but on that touchdown drive, Brian hit Jerame Tuman in the right-middle-back of the end zone to win it. It was a hard play-action pass roll-out, run-pass option that we scored on. I was more relieved than anything when we scored, because my quarterback had survived that day."

The touchdown was no accident, though. There were subtle adjustments made as the play unfolded to make it work. "We had run that play a lot during the year," Parrish recalls. "Chris Howard, our running back, made a good hard run-fake, and Brian had enough elusiveness on the corner to get outside. Tuman had a knack for getting open, and on that one, instead of running all the way to the corner, he saw them covering and kind of slowed down. He actually stopped in a little void back there, and Griese put it on him.

"Griese had a real calmness on that play," Parrish continues. "He made the defense cover every option we had. When Brian saw the one man he could get the ball to, he did. Brian was really good on that play."

Michigan went on to win the game 28-24 when Wolverine linebacker Sam Sword iced the outcome with an interception during Iowa's last-gasp drive. It saved a game that very well could have gotten away, and Michigan continued on to the Big Ten and national titles.

Nothing was guaranteed that season, though, until the Ohio State game. The finale was in Ann Arbor, and it brought another moment for Parrish that sticks with him like it happened yesterday. "I was right about the spot directly across from [Charles] Woodson before his punt return," Parrish says with a smile. "I remember thinking to myself, 'You know we haven't been very good on these returns this year. I mean we haven't run back a punt all year. This would be a heck of a time for it.' And lo and behold, down the same Desmond Howard sideline, against the same team, with the same results, Woodson did it. I think, without question, that was one of the great highlights in that Stadium."

Woodson's return helped the Wolverines to a 20-14 win over the Buckeyes, and they completed the regular season with an unblemished record. Parrish and the rest of the players and coaches moved on to the Rose Bowl and won that one, too, but for Parrish, the tales he will tell about that magical season will revolve around the magic at Michigan Stadium on those two Saturdays against Iowa and Ohio State.

"Brian Griese had a real calmness on that play."

It Just Came Natural!

In the story I just related, Stan Parrish talked about the "Desmond Howard" sideline. That reference came from the Ohio State game of 1991. In that game, Desmond Howard, on his way to the Heisman Trophy, just like Charles Woodson six years later, had returned a punt for a score that helped seal the game, and the Heisman. The big difference in the two runbacks was in the finish of each play. When Woodson scored, he was mobbed by his teammates. When Howard scored, he had the time to strike a Heisman Trophy-like pose in the end zone before being mobbed by his team.

Many thought the pose was a bit presumptuous of Desmond, but the situation almost begged for something like that. Howard was closing out a great year. He had established himself as the frontrunner for the award at about the midseason mark. Even the national television announcers mentioned the award in the play-by-play call. The great Keith Jackson, while calling the Howard return on ABC, said, "Goodbye Howard, hello Heisman," as Desmond crossed the goal-line amidst the roar of over 100,000 fans.

It was one of those great moments in Michigan Stadium, but Desmond told me recently that the pose after the score had been thought out long before that Saturday against Ohio State. "Actually, it was something that was brought to my attention earlier in the year by a teammate of mine," Howard says. "He wanted me to do something like that when we played up in Boston College. I had scored four touchdowns in that game, but I wasn't going to do anything then. It would have been like counting the chickens before the eggs hatch," Desmond laughed.

"Going into the Ohio State game," Howard remembers, "I thought to myself, I'm from Cleveland, this is the biggest rivalry in college football as far as any of us in the Midwest are concerned, so if I get in the end zone today, I've got to do something special. It just came natural to me. As soon as I broke the punt return and got into the end zone, it just came to me, and I hit the pose."

Of course, the fans and his teammates loved it. The newspaper photographers caught the pose at the time, and it became a national

Desmond Howard strikes the Heisman pose.

story. After all, he hadn't won the Heisman yet. Would there be a touch of backlash? Desmond says the aftermath from the coaching staff and others was minimal, "I don't think Coach Mo [head coach Garry Moeller] even saw it at the time," Desmond laughs. "He was just so happy that I scored and everything, he never even noticed. He didn't know until after the game about the pose."

Moeller must have been one of the few, because Desmond and the Heisman pose is a tale from Michigan Stadium that left an indelible mark on every Michigan football fan lucky enough to experience the moment that Saturday in Ann Arbor.

"Go Back to the Defense!"

Three Michigan players have won the Heisman Trophy. They were Tom Harmon, Desmond Howard, and Charles Woodson. The last to win it was Woodson in the 1997 season, and he may have been the most unique of the three. He played in the modern era of platoon football. He happened to be primarily a defensive player. Most Heisman winners come from the offensive side of the ball, and Woodson became the first ever to win it as a defensive player.

You could make the argument that Tom Harmon was also a defensive player who won the award, but he played in the days of one-platoon football. He played both offense and defense. And, to be honest, most of Harmon's exploits that were lauded at the time were from the offensive side of the ball. He passed, ran, kicked, returned kicks, and generally did everything for Michigan. He certainly was deserving of the Heisman, but Woodson's talents become as impressive when you remember he also played some offense, too, in an era when that isn't done.

There isn't any question that if Woodson did not play some offense, or return punts during that 1997 season, he probably wouldn't have won the Heisman. But he did, and the truth is, some of the Michigan coaches wanted to play Woodson a little more on offense than they did.

Erik Campbell coached the receiving corps in 1997, and he remembers the double duty Woodson had to pull during practice. "He'd come over from the defensive practice during the week," Campbell says, "and he was fun. He loved it. All Woodson wanted to know when he came over to the receivers from the defense was the game plan, what he had to do, and 'gimme the ball.' That's all he wanted to know," Campbell laughs. "He wanted to know how many times he'd get the ball, and if it wasn't enough, he'd get upset."

The preparation for Woodson moving over to wide receiver from his normal cornerback position started well before the season ever began. "We taught him the routes he needed to know during that summer," recalls Campbell, "and once he got all that offense figured out, we were ready. During game weeks, all he wanted to know was what route he was running, and when he was getting the ball. That's all he wanted to know! He was easy to coach. You'd tell him, 'Go down the field, turn around, and catch the ball. Once you catch it, make your magic happen,' and that's what he did."

The 1997 Ohio State game was the game that Woodson probably nailed down the Heisman because, like Harmon, he did everything that day. Campbell remembers it clearly, "That's the game he made three plays on offense, defense, and special teams," Campbell says. "We were struggling on offense, we needed to make a play, and his number was called. He knew the ball was going to him, and he came up with the play, and we won the game. When we called the play, Griese knew where to go with the ball. You go to the best player on the field! We did, and that's one of the reasons we won."

Woodson could have played even more offense than he did that year. The coaches had been discussing different ways to utilize his talents, but in one instance, Woodson himself declined the opportunity. Campbell remembers a practice one day behind Schembechler Hall. "He was a great athlete, and we wanted to get the ball in his hands," Erik says, "Woodson had to bounce between offense and defense, practicing both ways during the week. I remember we tried to play him at quarterback. We wanted him run a quarterback draw. Whenever we tried to do that, Woodson would say, 'Oh, my knee hurts, my knee hurts, I don't think I can do it.' Coach Carr got so

Charles Woodson makes the magic happen against Ohio State.

upset, he'd yell, 'Get out of there! Go back to the defense!' For some reason, he didn't want to do it," exclaims Campbell.

It may have been the only thing Charles didn't want to do that year. He did just about everything else for Michigan in that special season. It was his last as a Wolverine. Only a junior, Woodson had accomplished about all that he could in his college career, so he left Ann Arbor and moved on to the NFL with the Oakland Raiders.

The Greatest Player of the Century

Since we've been talking about Heisman Trophy winners, it's probably a good time to give the first Michigan Heisman winner his due. For those who remember Tom Harmon, ol' No. 98, there is no argument. He was the best. It is as simple as that.

For those who *played* with him, it's a slam dunk. Tom Harmon was the best ever, period. That is pretty high praise, but it comes from a man who knows. It comes from Harmon's teammate and backfield partner, Forest Evashevski.

In his lifetime, Evy has seen a lot of football. From his days at Michigan in the late 1930s to the rest of his career, which saw him achieve legend status in collegiate football circles, Evy knows talent. When I asked him in the fall of 2001 to remember his biggest thrill in Michigan Stadium during his playing career, Evashevski didn't hesitate. "The greatest thrill I had was starting as a sophomore and playing in front of Tom Harmon in the backfield. Tom Harmon was the greatest football player that we had in the whole century."

Evashevski said it in a very matter-of-fact way, and then went on to tell me why he believed it. "He ran, he passed, and he held the state record in the 100 in Indiana for 15 years. He was a good punter; he also kicked our field goals and extra points, and kicked off. And not only that, he was a great defensive back. Not many people know this about Harmon," Evy continued, "but after he left Michigan and joined the military, his plane was shot down during the war. His legs were so badly scarred from that incident that the doctors wouldn't let him play offense. So he went to the Los Angeles Rams in the pros and became a regular starter for them on *defense.*"

You simply are not going to convince Evy that anybody was any better than Harmon. Certainly, everyone who saw him play at Michigan Stadium would probably agree. But the measure of Harmon's greatness happened away from Michigan Stadium, according to Evashevski. "We were playing Ohio State in Columbus in 1940," Evy remembers fondly. "We had won the game 40-0. Tom's jersey was torn all the way off. He had no sleeves left on his jersey. When Tom came off the field, he got a standing ovation from the Ohio State crowd. When you get that from their fans and you're a Michigan man, it's pretty special. That was a great thrill for all of us."

If Evashevski's evaluation of Harmon isn't enough, there is more. Hercules Renda was a sophomore halfback for the Wolverines when Harmon came to Michigan as a freshman. "He was one of the best ever!" Renda echoes Evy. "He did it all. And remember this," Renda continues, "Harmon was six feet, two inches tall and about

Ol' No. 98, the greatest ever!

190 pounds. In those days our *whole team* averaged 180 pounds. He was one of the biggest guys on our team, and he had all that speed and natural ability, too."

Renda says that Harmon was not a prima donna either, despite his great talent. "He was just one of the boys. He was a great team player. He carried the team. He was fortunate to have Evy as a blocker, too. He was the ideal guy for Tom. They were like a pair of twins, Harmon and Evy. Class guys, on and off the field!"

Harmon of Michigan, the best ever. You will not get an argument from me.

"We Were Just Killing Them!"

Practice has always been fertile territory for great stories about Michigan football. Truth is, players spend a lot more time in practice interacting with coaches than they do in games. This is a story about practice at Ferry Field. It comes from one of Michigan's all-time greats, Roger Zatkoff.

Roger was a big, strong kid from Hamtramck, Michigan, when he enrolled at Michigan in 1949. He was also a fierce-hitting linebacker. One of the standard drills during a Monday practice in those days under coach Bennie Oosterbaan was to have freshmen come over and work with the varsity players who didn't see a lot of action in the previous Saturday's game. When Roger played, freshmen weren't allowed to compete at the varsity level, so it was an opportunity for the coaches to get a good look at the freshmen against upperclassmen in competition.

On this particular day, Oosterbaan wanted a couple of freshmen linebackers to work a tackling drill against the varsity. "When Oosty called for a couple of freshmen to work this tackling drill," Zatkoff says, "Ted Toper and I went over to the varsity field. Toper and I were pretty good-sized for those days, and Toper was actually bigger than I was. So, they put a couple of tackling dummies out on the field. They then handed the ball off to the halfback and told him to run between the dummies. 'Tope' and I were right behind the dummies, and we'd have a free shot at tackling them. They wanted to toughen these halfbacks up a little bit, so Toper and I worked them over pretty good. We had fun! We were just killing them!" Zatkoff laughs.

"The following day," Roger continued, "Oosty sends the manager over to the freshman practice and he says, 'Send two more guys over to the varsity for tackling drills, but *don't* send Zatkoff and Toper!' The manager said this to Cliff Keen, our freshmen coach. So Keen comes over to me and Toper and he says, 'You guys go.' We start running over to the varsity practice and get about halfway there when Oosterbaan sees us and yells, 'Go back, send two more. I don't want you guys here. You're going to kill us. We won't have anybody to play on Saturday.'"

Roger says today that it his one of his fondest memories of his days at Michigan. I'll bet for the varsity players that he and Toper tackled that afternoon, it wasn't such a fond memory.

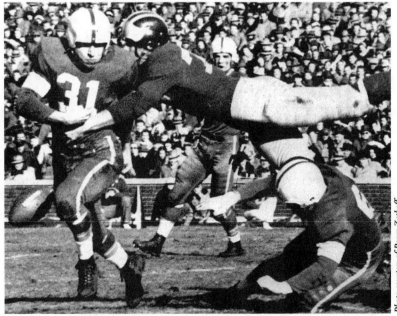

Roger Zatkoff flies at an opponent and causes a fumble.

The 10-10 Tie

In the 1973 season, Michigan and Bo Schembechler had a great football team. They went through the first 10 games of the season unbeaten and unchallenged. Their closest margin of victory during that 10-game stretch was 14 points. Going into their finale against Ohio State, they had allowed a total of 58 points, while scoring a total of 320. They were very good.

In the final game of the year against the Buckeyes, Michigan fell behind 10-0 in the first half. In the second half, though, the Wolverines were dominant but couldn't push across the winning score, and the game ended in a tie at 10. Ohio State, which had come into the game at Michigan Stadium ranked No. 1 in the country and unbeaten themselves, tied Michigan for the Big Ten title. Both teams finished with 10-0-1 season records. The Rose Bowl representative from the Big Ten would be determined by a vote of the conference athletic directors, because the Buckeyes and Wolverines had tied for the championship.

It was a foregone conclusion that Michigan would get the nod to go to the Rose Bowl. After all, Ohio State had gone the year before, and Michigan had been the dominant team in their head-to-head matchup for the majority of the game. Only one factor left Michigan fans in doubt as the athletic directors cast their ballots. Wolverine quarterback Dennis Franklin had broken his collarbone during the OSU game. It was unclear whether he would be fully recovered to participate in the Rose Bowl. Still, it wasn't that much of an issue, and Michigan was confident they would be heading to Pasadena.

The following Sunday morning, everyone in the Michigan football family was shocked when it was announced that the athletic directors had voted to send Ohio State to the Rose Bowl. The Wolverines were shut out from any bowl consideration. The Big Ten had a rule, at the time, that allowed only the conference champion to go to a postseason bowl, and that bowl was the Rose Bowl. So the Wolverines, an unbeaten conference championship team, would stay home on New Year's Day.

No one was more upset about the development than Schembechler himself. "To have that vote occur," Bo says, "shows that we had some very weak character guys in athletic director positions in the Big Ten. That's been proven.

"Everybody thought, ah well, we'll let it go and forget about it," Bo remembers. "But I had some great football players and great teams that never got to play in the great classic Rose Bowl. They were some of the great football teams in the United States of America. I never forgot that.

"I always said to myself," Bo continues, "if I ever let up on my bitterness over what happened to that football team in 1973, I'm not being fair to those guys who played. So I never have. And I've been bitter about it ever since, and I'll never forget it as long as I live."

While it has been tough for Schembechler to rationalize anything good resulting from the injustice, the years have given him some perspective. "Fortunately," Bo goes on, "as a result of that situation, we took the determination of the Rose Bowl representative out of the hands of the athletic directors because they weren't qualified to handle it. Second, because of that Michigan team in 1973, all these other teams in the Big Ten conference now have the opportunity to play in a postseason bowl game. The restriction by the Big Ten that it was the Rose Bowl or no bowl, which was as antiquated and stupid as anything the Big Ten's ever done, was eliminated.

"So we did accomplish something," Bo says philosophically, "but it came at a hell of an expense."

It did indeed. When you consider that the Schembechler teams of 1972 through 1974 finished with a combined record of 30-2-1 and never appeared in a bowl game, you can understand Bo's frustration. So while the 1973 game with Ohio State that ended in a 10-10 tie was one of those classics in Michigan Stadium, it was the aftermath that etches the game forever in Wolverine football history.

He Never Missed a Trick

It seems that a lot of the great stories surrounding Michigan Stadium just happen to include Ohio State. Maybe it's because of the rivalry. Who knows why, but it just seems that whenever Ohio State and Michigan get together, a story develops. Such is the case with the Friday before the Buckeyes and Wolverines met in 1977.

The weather for that November game was iffy. There was a forecast with a possibility of snow, so the field at Michigan Stadium was covered with a tarp. Michigan didn't practice in the Stadium that day, and neither would Ohio State. At least, that was the plan.

Michigan equipment manager Jon Falk was the man assigned to tell Woody Hayes, when he and his Buckeyes arrived, that the field was covered and practice would have to be cancelled. Jon recalls that Friday afternoon as he waited for Coach Hayes. "When he got off the bus at the Stadium, ready to practice, I walked up to him and said, 'Coach Hayes, just so you know, you're not going to be able to practice today. The field is covered because of the threat of snow. Michigan didn't practice, and you won't be able to either.' At that point," recalls Jon, "he grabbed me and jammed his index finger into my chest about five times, and he said, 'Every time I come to Michigan, all they want to do is screw me, screw me, screw me!'"

Falk laughs about it now, but at the time he had a job to do, so he responded, "'Yes sir, Coach, I know that, but you're still not going to be able to practice on that field.' Well, he went to the locker room with his team, and I'll be darned if he didn't get one of the guys who took care of the field to help him take the tarp off half of the field. He talked the guy into helping him pull the tarp halfway off the field, and by God, Coach Hayes took his team down on that field and practiced."

Jon says he was unaware of the practice until Ohio State was finished, so Falk went over and reported to Coach Schembechler. "I told Bo that Woody had gone over and pulled the tarp off and practiced anyway. Bo looked at me and laughed," recalls Falk.

"'He pulled the tarp and practiced anyway?' Bo asked. I said, 'He sure did.'"

According to Falk, Bo smiled and said, "The old man doesn't miss a trick, does he?" Jon responded, "He didn't miss one today, because he practiced and we didn't."

Coach Hayes happened to win that battle on Friday, but the next day Bo prevailed. The Wolverines beat the Buckeyes that Saturday 14-6 and won the Big Ten championship.

"We Thought We Had Arrived!"

It's amazing how many people talk about the lessons they've learned from coaches during their playing days at Michigan that have stayed with them through life. You can learn a lot about yourself while playing the game. Some coaches can help you with the lessons, and at Michigan, there may have been no coach better at teaching those life lessons than Bo Schembechler.

This story comes from tight end Derrick Walker, who learned one of those life lessons from Bo during the 1988 season. To understand this story, you also have to understand that Derrick Walker is a quality young man who had proven himself long before this event even took place.

As a young player for the Wolverines, Walker had suffered a severe knee injury. He had to undergo a knee reconstruction operation that, at the time, was a relatively new procedure. To be honest, the knee injury he suffered, in many instances, was considered career-ending. But Derrick was not about to let it stop him. He spent countless hours rehabilitating the knee and made it back from the injury and into the starting lineup. So Derrick had already exhibited that he was a dedicated and well-grounded young man.

Still, there were lessons to be learned, and for Derrick Walker one came after the Miami of Florida game in 1988. "Bo really didn't throw the ball to the tight ends that much during that time," Walker begins, "but Jeff Brown, the other tight end, and I had great games against Miami, even though we lost 31-30. I caught, like, five or six

Derrick Walker, blocker first, pass catcher second.

passes, and Jeff caught maybe four. We thought we had arrived. We both thought, hey, this may be our shot to make it to the pros.

"Even though we lost the game," Derrick remembers, "we were happy about our stats. I mean, for the tight ends to catch a combined nine passes was almost unheard of in the Bo days. So, we went to our meetings on Monday, still feeling good about ourselves, yet still upset about the loss. The first people Bo called out in the meeting were Jeff and me. Bo said, 'My tight ends *block*, they don't catch passes. You guys laid an egg in blocking even though you caught all those passes!'"

Derrick admits he was a bit surprised. "We thought we had played a good game," Walker recalls. "It just made an impression on me that Bo wasn't grooming players for the pros. He was grooming them for life. It was the kind of thing that I carried with me my entire career. You know, one day you are on top of the world and the next day you're not. Bo would always say, 'You either get better, or you get worse.'

"Bo was trying to teach us a lesson," Walker says. "I think he was happy with the way we played, but it was his way of keeping us grounded. It was a great experience, because Jeff and I thought we were big-timers after that. But when Bo called us out in front of the whole team, he taught me a lesson in life. Bo was good at that. He taught me that winning as a team was more important than individual success. It's something I've carried with me my entire life."

By the way, Derrick did make it to the pros. He had a fine career in the NFL. But it was that day at Michigan Stadium and the following Monday when he learned how to be a better player.

That Year Was a Disaster!

Throughout Bo Schembechler's coaching tenure at Michigan, there weren't many down years. Over 21 years at the helm of the Wolverines, he compiled a 194-48-5 record. With that kind of mark, you wouldn't imagine there would have been a tough year, but there was. In 1984, Michigan struggled to a 6-6 record. Even though they were invited to the Holiday Bowl and lost to eventual national champion Brigham Young in a tight game, it was subpar for a Bo-coached team.

In his entire career at Michigan, Bo never had a losing season. The Wolverine team of 1984 was the closest he ever came. If you ask him today about that season, Bo will say with a defiant smirk, "That year was a disaster, OK? Now let's move on!"

As the old saying goes, time heals all wounds, and the 1984 season has blended with the rest and doesn't diminish Bo's standing as one of the great ones in Wolverine history.

The co-captains of that team were Doug James and Mike Mallory. James was an offensive guard and a guy with a great personality. He is very humorous and can find a silver lining in any cloud. This tale from Michigan Stadium takes you inside the mind of Doug James, and inside a players-and-coaches-only reunion we had a few years ago.

After Bo had retired, a group of his former players got the idea to put together a reunion for all of Bo's teams. We called it, "Twenty-one Years, 21 Teams...Our Tribute to Bo." We commissioned an artist to create a bronze bust of Coach Schembechler. We presented it to him the night of the banquet. We got tremendous response for the event, too, as nearly 500 of Bo's former players and coaches made the trek to Ann Arbor from all over the country.

The players and coaches who had gathered formed a giant block "M" on the practice field outside of Schembechler Hall, and a picture was taken from high above on a crane for all of us to take home as a remembrance of the weekend. It was a great time for everyone.

When it came time for the banquet, a representative from every team spoke on behalf of his team. There were some great stories told, and laughter exploded from the room on a regular basis.

Dan Dierdorf had been selected as the emcee for the evening, and he was outstanding. If you remember Dan from his days on ABC's *Monday Night Football* broadcasts, you know he has a tremendous sense of humor and a very quick wit. He is also very good with the needle when it comes to trading good-natured barbs with friends or teammates. Among those who played for Bo at Michigan, good-natured barbs are pretty much standard operating procedure.

Anyway, as the event started that evening, Dan opened the program standing at the podium, gaveling the guys to order. He said, "Men, we have a motion on the floor from Reggie McKenzie that we throw the 1984 team out of the hall! We don't want a 6-6 team in here amongst us." With that, the entire group roared their approval.

Dan went on, "Can we see a show of hands for the motion?" Of course every hand in the place went skyward. At that point, Dan leaned down to Bo who was sitting on the dais right next to the podium. When he straightened back up, Dan announced, "Wait a minute, the coach has overruled us. The 1984 team can stay." Again, we all roared with laughter.

While all this was going on, Doug James was working his way through the mass of tables and players to a microphone set up in the audience area. When the laughter quieted, Dierdorf recognized James's intention to speak. Doug then addressed the gathered throng. "Go ahead, you guys laugh and make fun of the 1984 team as much as you want, but remember," Doug continued, "that season, our team led the nation...in attendance!"

It may have been the funniest line of the night. The entire room erupted with laughter, and we all gave Doug and his 1984 team a standing ovation.

While the 1984 squad has suffered some because of that so-called "down year," don't ever forget what the players on that team did the year before and the year after. In 1983, Michigan won nine games. They were invited to the Sugar Bowl and lost to Auburn 9-7 in one of the great defensive performances in Wolverine history. Auburn featured Bo Jackson, Lionel James, and Tommy Agee all in the same Wishbone backfield. Michigan did not allow Auburn to cross their goal-line that night. Auburn barely missed the national title that year, and many thought they should have won it, but Michigan played them to a standstill.

In 1985, the Wolverines rebounded from their previous season by winning 10 games. They were selected to play Nebraska in the Fiesta Bowl and beat the Cornhuskers 27-23.

Many of the Wolverines on these teams also played on that 1984 team. So we shouldn't be too fast to take shots at our brethren of 1984. They added plenty to the rich tradition of Michigan.

Doug James (No. 73) leads the sweep and leads the attendance figures.

The Guy Ran the Gauntlet!

The longer I worked on these stories, the more interesting it became. To reminisce about my days at Michigan with friends or other Wolverine players became a real highlight of my day. Such was the case when I tracked down Rob Lytle, and we had a laugh-filled conversation over the phone.

Rob was a great tailback and fullback in the mid-1970s. He scored 29 career touchdowns and still ranks sixth on Michigan's all-time leading rushers list. In addition, he is a wonderful guy with an even more wonderful sense of humor. So when I asked him to relate a tale or two of his from Michigan Stadium, Lytle jumped right into it.

"When I was in school," Lytle recalls with a laugh, "streaking had become the rage. This particular incident happened during spring practice. It was a typical Saturday. We were scrimmaging in the Stadium. It was a halfway nice day, sunny out, and we were working hard. As usual, Bo [Schembechler] wasn't happy with anything we were doing. He was screaming and ranting and raving. All of a sudden, from the top of the Stadium at the north end, a guy came down the steps, hopped the wall, and ran right down the middle of the field, between the offensive and defensive huddles, continued to the other end of the field, hopped the wall, ran back up the steps and out the exit. *He was naked as a jaybird!*"

After Rob and I stopped laughing, Lytle continued this amazing tale. "Everybody just stopped and looked. We were in shock. Nobody stopped him or anything; we all just stood there and stared. I mean practice *stopped*! There wasn't anybody in the stands except for maybe a few parents of a couple of players. We really didn't notice this streaker until he reached the field, but once we did notice, everything and everybody stopped and stared at this guy.

"I mean, we were just finishing up a play and wandering back to the huddle around the 40-yard line," Lytle said between laughs, "and he just ran the gauntlet, *right through the whole team!* I think a few guys came out of their shock and applauded. It wasn't like a standing ovation or anything. For the most part we all just stood there with our mouths open!"

At this point, I wondered what in the world was Bo's reaction to this streaker? Rob told me the coach's reaction is the best part of the story. "After this guy disappeared through the exit at the other end of the Stadium," Rob went on, "we were kind of milling around chuckling, and wondering what was coming next from Bo. He didn't disappoint us. After the guy disappeared through the exit, Bo growled, 'See that, even the fans think you stink!'"

I guarantee Bo thought the whole incident was hilarious, too. He had to get a laugh out of it. He probably just didn't want anybody to know during practice. Anyway, that's the great untold (until now) story of the streaker at Michigan Stadium. As Lytle puts it in his own charming way, "That sure sticks in my mind as a great day in Michigan football!"

Lytle (No. 41) streaks downfield in his uniform.

"Are We This Good?"

We go back to the broadcast booth for the next tale. Since 1972, on and off, I have been broadcasting or covering Michigan football. I have been very lucky in that regard. Over the years, you remember games and plays; often, you forget what year and other details, but there are some moments that stay with you. Such is the case with the Penn State vs. Michigan game in 1997.

Frank Beckmann and I were broadcasting the game for WJR Radio and the statewide network. It was a highly anticipated game. Both the Nittany Lions and the Wolverines were unbeaten as they squared off at Beaver Stadium in State College. Penn State was actually ranked ahead of the Wolverines entering the game. The Lions were ranked third in the country, and the Wolverines were fourth.

We were expecting a tight game that would go down to the wire. Two plays in this game, and an unspoken realization that passed between Frank and me, are the moments I will never forget as long as I continue to broadcast football.

Early in the game, Penn State completed a pass. It was a throwback tight end screen. As the Penn State player roared downfield, he started to pass the Penn State bench. He was right near the sideline. Out of nowhere, Wolverine defensive back Daydrion Taylor, like he was shot out of a cannon, hurled his body at a dead sprint into the ball carrier and just blasted him backwards and out of bounds right in front of Joe Paterno and the rest of the Penn State bench.

There was an audible gasp from the entire crowd. The hit by Taylor was that ferocious. Both players were injured and stayed down. After a few frightening moments, both players got up and moved to their benches. The Penn State crowd applauded both, as they appeared to be OK. I thought at the time that Taylor had just made a statement play. When the Penn State bench witnessed this hit right in front of them, it appeared as though they moved back, almost as if they didn't want to get too close to Taylor. He had sent them all a message that on this day Michigan was committed, body and soul, to the effort ahead.

As it turned out, that was Daydrion Taylor's last play as a football player. While he was briefly knocked unconcious by his effort, he was able to recover and walk unassisted to the bench. But he had injured his neck and was advised that playing football was no longer an option for him.

Taylor may not have played another down, but on that one play, he ignited his entire team. His hit will forever stay with me as one of the defining moments of that season. As far as I'm concerned, Taylor also belongs high on the list of impact players in Michigan football history.

After Taylor's play, the game completely turned, and Michigan dominated. It wasn't even close. Penn State could not move the ball, and the Wolverines could not be stopped. Michigan's lead kept growing. Then, with Michigan driving again, Charles Woodson, Michigan's great defensive back, came into the game as a receiver. Frank, handling the play-by-play, caught the substitution immediately. I can almost repeat the broadcast verbatim. Beckmann said, "Woodson splits to a slot left, Tai Streets is split wide outside of Woodson. Griese calls the signals. *They've got single coverage on Woodson!*" Frank exclaimed, and then went on, "Griese takes the snap, he's back to throw. Woodson is behind the safety, Griese's got him, 15, 10, five... TOUCHDOWN MICHIGAN!"

The Woodson score made it a 17-0 Michigan lead, and we were still in the *first half.* After the extra point, Frank threw to a commercial break. We sat in the press box and looked at each other without saying a word for about five seconds. Finally, I took off my headset and said to him, "Are you thinking what I'm thinking?"

Frank responded, "I think so. What are you thinking?"

"Are we this good?" I asked.

Frank smiled, looked up at the scoreboard and said, "I'm thinking the same thing, and yeah, I think we are this good!"

Over the years, we've had conversations during games like that before, but both of us had always had reservations about this or about that. In this game, neither of us had any reservations. It was the most impressive performance by a Michigan team against a quality opponent that we had ever witnessed.

Daydrion Taylor (No. 28) makes another impact play.

We also happened to be right about how good the Wolverines were. Penn State got hammered that day, 34-8. Michigan finished the year unbeaten. Along the way, seven of their 12 wins came against ranked teams. Four of those seven were ranked in the top 10. After beating Washington State in the Rose Bowl, the Wolverines were tapped as the national champions.

Rodgers and Hammerstein

They tell me that it is a classic. I'm not so sure I agree, but if those fine folks who are regular listeners of Michigan football on WJR radio want to call it a classic, then so be it. Who am I to argue?

This classic does not refer to a game. It does not refer to a play. It refers to a radio broadcast of a Michigan game in Michigan Stadium. If this had happened during a television broadcast, it would be called a blooper. But it happened during a radio broadcast, and over the years it has stayed in the memories of our faithful listeners, so it is referred to by some as a classic.

In the mid-1980s Michigan was battling Northwestern on a beautiful Saturday in Ann Arbor. The Wolverines had a fine team, and they were beating the Wildcats handily. Michigan had a particularly strong defensive line this season, and two of the regulars in that defensive line were Mike Hammerstein and Nate Rodgers.

As the game progresses and Michigan's lead builds, Beckmann and I are doing our best to keep the momentum going from a broadcast perspective. As the game gets to blowout proportions, I have to admit, the announcers try to keep the entertainment level high, even though the game, for all intents and purposes, is over. I've always felt that, as an announcer, you work harder during a blowout than you do during a tight game. During those tight games, your focus stays sharp. Every play is important. Strategy remains an issue on every down, and you are strategizing in the broadcast booth just as the coaches are on the sideline. It's truly a great ride during a tight game.

If the game gets out of hand, the broadcast mind begins to lose just a touch of focus. Every play isn't as important. Sometimes, you begin watching the scoreboard for the scores of other games being played that day. You try what you can to keep the folks out there listening, even though the outcome has been decided. Such was the case this particular Saturday as Michigan was drubbing Northwestern, and Frank Beckmann and I were doing our best to keep the folks at home entertained.

Somewhere in the second half, Northwestern had the football and they called a pass play. The Wolverine defense swarmed in and sacked the Wildcat quarterback. As the pile of players on the poor Northwestern quarterback began to get up, I was thinking of a comment to use and explain the particular blitz Michigan had used to achieve the sack, when I heard Frank closing out his play-by-play call. "And, as they unpile," Frank related with enthusiasm, "Nate Rodgers and Mike Hammerstein get up from the bottom. They each got in there for the sack. Oh my," Frank continued, "Rodgers and Hammerstein, what a melodious tune they played for the Michigan defense."

I turned and looked at Frank. He turned and looked at me. He started to laugh. I looked back at the field, chuckling, and said something like, "You've been waiting for that all year, haven't you?" Frank didn't respond.

I looked back at him. Frank was leaning back in his seat, laughing uncontrollably. The Rodgers and Hammerstein line had just cracked his funny bone. *He couldn't talk!* He was pointing at me, through tears of laughter, indicating I should continue. I was in a little better shape than he was, so I called the play-by-play for the next play, a Northwestern punt. I remember saying something about why Frank couldn't continue, just so the listeners wouldn't wonder why he had disappeared.

As the game continued, Frank got himself back together. He was still right on the edge of breaking up, though, when he returned to the microphone. At that point, a comment flashed into my mind. As he began to speak, I blurted out, "Man, I'm sure glad we're not playing Oklahoma!"

Well, that did it for both of us. Frank, through his laughter, looked at me and said on the radio, "How could you!" With that, both of us erupted with the giggles. We must have missed three or four plays. We tried, but if you were listening that day, you must have been clairvoyant if you figured out what happened during the next few plays.

I don't know why I made the Oklahoma comment. I didn't even know that Richard Rodgers and Oscar Hammerstein wrote *Oklahoma!* It just seemed like the thing to do at the time.

We came to our senses a few moments later and finished the game. Afterwards, in the parking lot, a lot of people came up to me and commented about the Rodgers and Hammerstein episode. Frank got the same reaction. Apparently, folks listening on their radios in the stadium got as much of a laugh out of it as we did.

The famous Rodgers and Hammerstein call is now in the archives at WJR. I also understand that there are always a couple of requests during the football season to replay it. The staff at WJR dutifully obliges, and we relive this classic a couple of times a year.

Meanwhile, Frank and I can only hope that Michigan never recruits any kids with the names Lerner and Loewe, or Gilbert and Sullivan, or Andrew Lloyd Webber.

Jim Brandstatter and Frank Beckmann, a very un-melodious pair.

It Was 75 Percent of His Highlight Film

Every now and again, Michigan Stadium plays host to great performances by an opponent of the Wolverines. We haven't discussed too many of those performances in this collection, but two quarterbacks from visiting teams put on a pair of exceptional displays that shouldn't be overlooked.

In 1998, following Michigan's national championship season, the Wolverines opened the year with two straight losses. Notre Dame beat Michigan in South Bend in the opener, and Syracuse stunned the Wolverines at Michigan Stadium in the home opener. In that Syracuse game, quarterback Donovan McNabb was unstoppable. Whenever the Orangemen needed a play, McNabb made one. Whether it was hitting a pass or scrambling out of trouble and making a play with his legs, McNabb did it. He was the best player on the field that day, and the Wolverines fell 38-28.

As I left the broadcast booth after McNabb's performance, I overheard a longtime Michigan fan say it was the best performance by an opposing quarterback in Michigan Stadium since Roger Staubach.

Staubach, of course, was the Heisman Trophy winner who played for the Naval Academy in the early 1960s. His performance against Michigan in 1963 left fans at Michigan Stadium in awe. One of the people who got an up-close and personal look at that performance was Wolverine defensive end Jim Conley.

"It was absolutely a great performance," Conley remembers. "That game was probably 75 percent of his entire highlight film for that year when he won the Heisman Trophy."

There were two plays in the game that Conley remembers specifically as vintage Staubach. "I played defensive end," Conley said. "And I beat a fullback around end on a pass play. I hit Staubach as hard as I could, and as he was going down, he flipped a pass off to his safety-valve receiver, and the guy ran for a touchdown."

Conley thought he had a sack on "Roger the Dodger," only to be thwarted by the Midshipmen's uncanny ability to make

Jim Conley (No. 82) chased Staubach around more than the Army.

something out of nothing. The nickname, "Roger the Dodger," was definitely appropriate, according to Conley.

"Jocko Nelson, our coach, had come up with this defensive scheme for the game," Conley remembers. "As a defensive end, Nelson wanted us to take three slow steps upfield. It was almost as if we were doing ballet. He wanted to make sure we contained Staubach. We wanted to keep him from scrambling.

"Anyway," Conley continues, "on this one play, I took my three slow steps, and I had a shot at Roger. I took the shot and missed him. He ran around me. I got off the ground and went back at him. Staubach cut back, right at me, and I missed him again. He then ran around the other end. So I got up again and started to take a pursuit angle to catch him. Wouldn't you know, he cut back again about 20 yards downfield right in the middle of the field, and I missed him again!

"So on one play, I missed Staubach three times!" Conley laughs. "I ran into Staubach many years later at the College Football Hall of Fame dinner. We talked about the game in 1963, and I told him that the least he could have done was give me a credit on his highlight film. After all," Conley chuckled, "I had more time on that film than he did!"

The following year, Conley got a measure of revenge against Staubach. The Wolverines won the 1964 game in Ann Arbor 21-0. Conley and Bill Yearby, an outstanding defensive lineman who played next to Conley, were chasing Staubach on another scramble, but this time they caught him. "We tackled him hard on the play," Conley says. "It was a clean hit, but he hurt his ankle, and that was the end of his year. He was never back to the way he was for rest of the season."

Still, Conley will never forget what Staubach did in 1963 to his Wolverines. "I would say," Conley states, "that Staubach's performance was the most exceptional day I've ever seen someone have against us."

"He Had Flames Coming Out of His Eyes!"

Jim Conley has a wealth of stories from his years at Michigan. As the captain of the 1964 Big Ten and Rose Bowl champion teams, Conley was in on a lot of memorable moments. One of these moments occurred against Northwestern in the 1964 championship season, and it involved his teammate, Bill Yearby.

"We were playing Northwestern," Conley recalls, "and Yearby, who played right next to me on the defensive line, and was on his way to becoming an All-American the next year, was, for some reason, really fired up for the game. I mean, he had flames coming out of his eyes!"

Conley says even the coaches were aware of Yearby's state of mind. "[Head coach Bump Elliott] came up to me before the game," Conley says, "and told me to keep an eye on Bill because he was so fired up.

"So we lined up for the first offensive play by Northwestern," Conley recalls, "and their tackle flew offsides and hit Yearby. They got a five-yard penalty, but Yearby was really upset. On the next play, this guy fires offsides and hits Yearby again! Now Bill is really jacked up. So I looked at Bill and told him, 'As soon as they line up, *we go!*'

"So Northwestern breaks the huddle and lines up for the next play," Conley remembers with a laugh, "and as soon as the quarterback walked up to the center, Yearby and I jumped offsides and knocked that tackle head over heels, right on his ass!"

This was quite a start to the ball game, and Conley says the referees decided to get things back under control. "Since I was the captain," Conley said, "the referee called me over with the Northwestern captain and said, 'This has got to stop.' So I said, 'They started it!' And the referee looked at me and said, '*I'm not talking to my children here!*'" Conley exploded with laughter as he related the story.

Well, the game carried on in a civilized manner the rest of the way. But Conley feels, to this day that Northwestern had a game plan focusing on Yearby. "They wanted to take Bill out of the game. They wanted him to retaliate and get taken out of the game."

Yearby and Conley spoiled the Wildcat plan, though, and the Wolverines dominated the game, winning 35-0.

"You're My Guy"

One of the great moments in recent history at Michigan Stadium came in Lloyd Carr's first year as head coach. Carr was the interim coach at the time, and it was the season of 1995. The Wolverines opened the campaign at home in the "Pigskin Classic," against a very good Virginia team. The Cavaliers had the likes of Tiki Barber at running back, and his twin brother, Ronde, was an outstanding cornerback. As the game progressed, things did not look good for the Wolverines. Virginia played very well, and Michigan could not move the ball. Heading into the fourth quarter, it looked like a lost cause. The Wolverines were down 17-0.

Going into the game there were a lot of question marks for Michigan, not the least of which was opening the season with a brand new quarterback. Coach Carr had waited until a week before the game to announce the starter, and it was sophomore Scott Dreisbach who got the call. In reality, Dreisbach knew a long time before anybody else that he would get the start. "I had told Scott during training camp that he was going to be our starter," Coach Carr recalls. "We really struggled in the first half of that game," Lloyd says. "I can't recall that we even made a first down. But I told Scott, when we left the locker room at the half, 'Find a way to win!' And he did!"

He did indeed. In the most remarkable comeback ever in Michigan Stadium, Dreisbach led Michigan to three touchdowns in the last 12 minutes for an 18-17 win. The last score came on a perfect pass from Dreisbach to Mercury Hayes in the corner of the end zone as the clock ticked to zero.

For his part, Dreisbach remembers not only the good in that game, but also the bad. "I remember the first interception I threw in that game was to Ronde Barber," Scott laughs.

At the time, he was a little more serious, and he remembers that Coach Carr really had an impact on his performance in the second half. "He told me," Scott recalls, "that he had all the confidence in the world in me. I should settle down and play the way he knew I could play. The first half was not a good half for my confidence in my first half of football as the Michigan starter. But Coach Carr said, 'You're my guy, go out there and do what I know you can do.'"

Through the third quarter the situation for Michigan hadn't gotten much better, and there were some fans who weren't sure that Dreisbach should still be in the game. A great many of the faithful had left for the parking lot and their tailgate parties. It was a test for both Dreisbach and Carr. Neither of them wavered, according

Mercury Hayes makes the catch that beats Virginia.

to Scott. "Coach Carr kept telling me, 'You don't have to look over your shoulder. You are my quarterback, and you are going to play.' So I went into that fourth quarter with confidence."

That confidence Coach Carr had in Dreisbach may have been the difference in the game, because Scott threw three touchdown passes to rescue the victory.

The first two touchdown throws are kind of vague in his memory, but the third one is anything but. "I remember it so vividly," Dreisbach says, "it gives me chills to this day whenever I watch it or think about it.

"It was a double-shake on each side," recalls Scott. "I had Amani [Toomer] to my left, and Mercury to my right. The pre-snap read was that Amani was going to be the guy I'd throw to. When I went back to throw, they doubled Amani, so at the end of my drop I knew I had to go to Mercury. I just put it out there, tried to keep it in bounds and let Mercury make a play on it. He ran a great route and kept his feet in bounds. It was very tight, but he made a great catch."

Although the crowd that day was over 100,000, there weren't that many in the stands for the finish. After Hayes's catch, the official hesitated for a moment before signaling touchdown while he conferred with another official. As soon as his arms went up, Dreisbach says it was wild. "It seemed like forever for the referee to put up his arms for a touchdown. It was a great feeling. Everybody at the Stadium went crazy.

"The next thing I remember," Dreisbach continues, "our bench just cleared, and there was a big pile of players in the end zone. I remember trying to stay away from the pile. I didn't want to be crushed by anybody!" Scott chuckles. "Remember it was so hot that day, a lot of us had heat exhaustion. We were cramping up throughout the game. I didn't want to get near the pile. I was exhausted!"

Everybody was drained after that finish, fans and players alike. I don't blame Dreisbach a bit for watching from a distance. He had been through a lot that afternoon. He'd suffered through the heat, a few boo-birds, a tough Virginia defense, and an internal battle with himself. Scott emerged from all of that with a memory nobody can take away. It was a come-from-behind win for the ages that he orchestrated in a great stadium that is full of great moments.

That sophomore year was Dreisbach's best season. Injuries and other factors cost him playing time in his junior and senior years. But he remains one of those special names that are woven into the fabric of the Michigan football tradition. I'm not overstating anything either; Coach Carr will back me up on it. "Scott Dreisbach and Mercury Hayes will always be special guys in my heart," Carr says, "because nobody who follows Michigan football will ever forget what they did in those last 12 minutes. I know I sure won't."

"I'll Tell You What I Could Have Had!"

Unforgettable performances at Michigan Stadium are abundant. Individuals who seize the moment are a special breed of cat. In most instances, these performances come from the stars or All-Americans. But there are also performances that come from the unexpected player.

Don't get me wrong, these unexpected heroes are very good, but for one reason or another, they haven't gotten the headlines. They have been making plays their entire careers, but they just haven't elevated themselves into the star category. Except for that one day when the heavens align, and they have a performance for the ages. Such is the case of Barry Pierson.

Barry Pierson is a native of St. Ignace, Michigan. As a matter of fact, Barry still lives there. On one Saturday in November 1969, Barry Pierson had a day in Michigan Stadium that Tom Harmon, Fritz Crisler, or any other Michigan legend would have been hard-pressed to match. It was against Ohio State in the famous 24-12 Wolverine victory. That day, Barry Pierson, of little St. Ignace, Michigan, was the best player on the field despite the fact that All-Americans littered both rosters.

If you've followed Michigan football, you know that Ohio State was considered the best college football team ever assembled that season. All Pierson did was intercept three Buckeye passes and return a punt nearly 60 yards to set up one of Michigan's touchdowns. He was the key player in the Wolverine defensive effort that shutout the Buckeyes' vaunted offense for the entire second half.

Barry's play that day was remarkable, but if you ask him about it today, he downplays his individual effort and focuses the attention on everybody else, "I was not the man that day," Barry says modestly. "What I did was my job. If you go through that film with a fine-tooth comb, you're going to see an awful lot of guys doing things right in order to beat Ohio State. I mean, there were some great plays, including offense, defense, and special teams. It was just good timing on my part."

Pierson is like that. Very modest, just a regular guy, but I had to press him. I reminded him of his three interceptions, and he interrupted me. "I'll tell you exactly what I could have had," Barry said with a laugh. "You're always looking for the perfect scenario, you know, so listen to this. [Tom] Curtis [the Michigan safety and Pierson's good friend] stole one from me. I dropped two more on down-and-out dives. That adds up to six, so when you think about it, I was really only 50 percent for the day. How does that sound?" Barry chuckled.

Nonetheless, the three he did intercept were huge. It was the last one he remembers most, though, and not because it was such a great play, rather, because of how it relates to today's football. "It doesn't show much on the film," Barry recalled, "but I actually covered a lot of ground to intercept the ball. If you compared that interception to today's standards, I never would have gotten there! They throw the ball so much harder today. I think you had a little more time in those days to react than they do now. Quarterbacks today look defensive backs off, then whip the ball in there a lot harder. I know that. It makes it harder on a defensive back these days, because you can't get the jump on it."

Despite the changes in the game from then to now, Barry Pierson still has those three interceptions locked in his memory. So do thousands of Michigan fans. They also have the memory of that

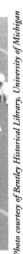

*Barry Pierson (No. 29), in the middle of his punt
return that sunk the Buckeyes in 1969.*

victory over Ohio State, which to Pierson wasn't as surprising as it was to some others. "You know, everybody says Bo did this, and Bo did that, but in our minds there was no way we were going to lose that game," Barry went on. "Bo told us that from day one. He showed us how we were going to win it, and that's exactly how we won it. I give most of the credit to Bo and his staff. They had that thing figured out perfectly."

So did you, Barry. So did you.

Good Play, Mike!

Back in the 1950s, the recruiting wars for high school athletes that we see today didn't exist. Back then, there was no ESPN cable television. There were no all-day all-sports talk radio stations. When a high school player committed to a university to play football, there was very little fanfare. About the only people who knew the entire recruiting class were the coaches.

With that environment in mind, let me relate a story from Terry Barr.

Barr, one of Michigan's all-time great players, came in with a very talented class. "We had no idea who was going to be on our team when we got down to Michigan as freshmen," said Barr. "There might have been a little something in the paper, but I never read anything. I heard, though, that we had a kid on our team who was an All-America high school player. So, I go out to practice and there is this guy out there, I mean he's·a monster, leaping over tall buildings in a single bound! You know, stay out of his way, he's mean, he's all those things. So, I'm saying to myself, this must be the All-American. I had never met him, but I knew he was from the U. of D. (University of Detroit High) and his name was Mike.

"If we had an All-American, this was the guy!" Terry laughs. "So, for the first two days of practice, I'm saying, 'Good play, Mike! Way to go, Mike,' you know, things like that. Well, about the second day of practice, Mike looked at me, and said, '*Hey, I'm not Mike! My name is Ron Kramer. Quit calling me Mike!*'

"What did I know?" Barr chuckled. "I mean if we had an All-American, it had to be Mike. I thought Kramer had to be Mike!"

Barr found out in a hurry about Kramer, and they are good friends to this day, despite the mistaken identity. Both of them went on to brilliant careers at Michigan and later in the NFL. But it was their shared experience in Ann Arbor that bonds them for life. Terry is unabashedly proud of his ties with Michigan, and he says the allure of the Maize and Blue struck him at a very early age. "I remember the Rose Bowl game of 1948," Terry recalls. He was in his early teens. "There was no TV, so I listened to it on the radio. That's when Michigan beat up on Southern Cal. I was glued to the radio. You can't imagine sitting there the whole time listening to the radio, but I did. It would have been fun to watch it, but it was great fun just listening to them run over S-C."

It wasn't long after that game that Terry Barr got to see his Wolverines in person. "The first game I ever saw Michigan play," Terry told me with reverence, "was against Ohio State. I went to Ann Arbor with a friend of mine. I had never been in the Stadium. I just couldn't believe it. I couldn't quit talking about it. I'm sure I was

Terry Barr makes an acrobatic catch for his beloved Wolverines.

pretty boring to some people, but how could you *not* be impressed?
I was 17 years old, and I walked all over that place."

Michigan Stadium had a profound effect on Terry Barr. He
wasn't finished being awed by the Stadium. Its magical quality still
had an impact on Barr when he finally realized his dream and suited
up to run out of the tunnel as a Michigan Wolverine. "It was one
thing to go out to practice," Barr says, "but it's a whole different
ball game when it's game time. When I think back on it, I hardly
remember my feet touching the ground."

Barr isn't alone in his memories of that first time running out
of the tunnel and into the Stadium. The same feelings run deep in

all of those who played there. They may be expressed differently, but it truly is a magical place.

Terry Barr is a guy who has accomplished a great many things in his life: a great collegiate football career, a great professional football career. He is a dedicated family man and an immensely successful businessman. You might think that Michigan is a distant memory, but you would be way off base, according to Barr. "I'll tell you right now, when people talk to me, and ask where I went to school, I mean, I am so proud, I can't wait to get it out of my mouth that I went to Michigan. And it's been that way with me since forever. It's an unbelievably special place."

"Will You Ease Off?"

It isn't very often that an official talks to a player during a game about how the player is playing the game. It happens, don't get me wrong, but for the most part, whatever an official might say, it usually pertains to a possible foul. For instance, if you're in the offensive line, you might walk by an official and he'll say, "Watch your hands, keep them inside." Or if you are a split end and you need to be off the line of scrimmage, you'll look at the linesman to see if you're back far enough off the line of scrimmage and he'll nod. Often, the captains will talk to the officials about accepting or declining penalties, but for the most part officials stay out of the way and certainly don't offer a lot of advice.

This is the tale of a time when an official did offer some advice. It comes from Roger Zatkoff, one of the Wolverines' best ever linebackers.

It was the final game at Michigan Stadium in the 1952 season. Michigan was battling Purdue. "In those days," Roger begins, "you could chuck an end as he's coming across the middle. I am really beating up on this end from Purdue. So in the third quarter, the referee comes to me and says, 'Will you ease off on this guy?'

"I said, 'What do you mean?' And he said, 'You're killing that kid.'"

Roger laughs about the exchange and says he wasn't sure what to do next. After a moment's hesitation Roger asked, "'Am I doing anything illegal?' The ref said, 'No, just ease off on him a little, will you?'" I mean, this guy wasn't catching anything in Roger's area, and Roger wasn't going to let him catch anything.

The next question was begging to be asked. "Did you ease off?" I asked Roger.

"Hell no," Roger responded as I expected.

"If you talk to the guys I played with," Roger continued, "they'll pretty much tell you that I had a habit of going to the ball. It didn't make any difference who was in my way. In college or in pro, if you were in my way, you were going to get hit. When I went to Green Bay, they actually called me 'Zany Zatkoff.' I figured if I was able to give myself up and get two of theirs, it was OK."

Roger got more than his share, certainly, during his career, and in that Purdue game, he helped the Wolverines to a 21-10 win. The Purdue end, by the way, didn't have a very good game thanks to Zatkoff. There was a reason, though, that Roger was intent upon having a great game that day. It was his last game in Michigan Stadium.

"To me," Roger said, "winning that game was a highlight. I mean, my four years at Michigan just flew by. The realization that this was it, you were never going to be playing in this Stadium again, made it special." Roger then started to laugh, and finished, "And frankly, I had fun that day against Purdue!"

"I Just Kind of Lost It!"

Following in the tradition of great linebackers who like to hit people, Ron Simpkins comes to mind as a Wolverine who followed in Zatkoff's footsteps. Simpkins still holds the career record for tackles in a season. In the mid-1970s he was a stand-out, and interestingly enough, Ron told me a tale from Michigan Stadium that included talking also. It must be a linebacker thing.

Anyway, the year was 1977. Michigan was ranked third in the nation, and they were hosting Texas A&M, the fifth-ranked team in the country. It was a highly anticipated matchup. It wasn't often that the Big Ten and the Southwest conferences got together in the regular season, so this was a red-letter game.

Simpkins tells me he was at an emotional peak for this game. "They had the great backfield of George Woodard and Curtis Dickey, and a quarterback that ran like a 9.3 in the 100," Ron remembers. "I guess it must have been the first really big game I played in, and I was really emotional. So we're going on the field, and I just kind of lost it that game! I started talking to Texas A&M the whole game, and I didn't stop."

Simpkins says today that he's not sure what came over him, but he was really dishing it out. "I told them, 'This is Michigan! You're never going to beat Michigan at home! This is our place!' And, you know, we weren't supposed to talk!" Ron laughs about it today but says he went off on A&M anyway.

Michigan crushed the Aggies that day, 41-3. It was a huge victory, but Simpkins says his behavior during the game did not go unnoticed. "When we went out to practice on Monday," says Simpkins, "every coach, offense and defense, comes to me and asks, 'Ron, were you talking on the football field?' I told them I seemed to recall a couple of things I might have said," Simpkins remembers sheepishly.

According to Simpkins, the coaches knew the whole story and didn't let him off the hook. "'Ron, you were talking the whole game'" Simpkins recalls them saying. "'We don't talk like that here at Michigan.' I got lectured by every coach on the field. They lectured me about Michigan football. What you do and what you don't do during the course of a game. I was player of the game that day, too."

Simpkins says it was just one of those things, but he also had a good reason for his behavior, too. "I was just so emotional. I mean, Texas A&M was coming in and threatening our territory."

That's Michigan Stadium to Ron Simpkins. It was his territory. He had to protect it, and he did.

"You Don't Walk in Here and Tell Me What You're Gonna Do!"

One of the great athletes that Michigan had on Bo Schembechler's early teams was Jim Betts. The truth of the matter is that Jim could have played just about anywhere. Receiver, quarterback, defensive back, anywhere in the lineup, Betts would have been successful. The problem for Betts was that he played quarterback in 1969. So did Don Moorehead.

Moorehead just happened to be the starter, so Betts didn't get to play that much. Moorehead and Betts also happened to be in the same class, which meant playing time for Betts in his senior season looked limited. As good as Jim was, he should have been playing somewhere, so in his senior year, Betts took matters into his own hands.

"We had lost Tom Curtis, Barry Pierson, and Brian Healy out of the secondary through graduation," Betts recalls. "The only guy coming back was Thom Darden, and I thought, 'I'm not going to sit on the pine another year, so I think I'll go over and play defense.' I talked to defensive backfield coach Dick Hunter first and told him I wanted to play safety. Hunter said, 'Hell yeah, bring your ass over here!'" says Jim, laughing.

The biggest hurdle Betts would have to overcome, though, was head coach Schembechler. "I went to his office and said, 'Bo, I'm going to move over to the defense and play safety for my senior year.' Bo looked at me and said, 'I'll be a son of a bitch. You don't walk in here and tell me what you're gonna do! You are my quarterback!' I came right back and said, 'No, Moorehead is your quarterback, I back him up.' Bo said, 'Same damn difference!'"

Jim Betts (No. 23) returns an interception against Ohio State in 1970.

As you can imagine, Jim Betts exhibited great courage going in to Bo and standing his ground. "I told Bo," Betts remembers, "'I am not going to sit on the bench this year. I'm going to go play defense.' Bo responded to me by saying, 'I'll tell you what you're going to do. You're going to play both damn positions!'"

Betts says he knew at that point he was winning the battle, so he said, "I don't care, that's fine with me. All I know is I'm not sitting on the bench again." Bo thought for a moment, and Jim says he waited anxiously for what Bo would say next. Finally, Bo spoke, "You better be ready to go when you have to go in, you got it?"

Jim said he felt relieved that he had won his point, but he couldn't leave it at that. Betts and Bo had a wonderful relationship. They genuinely enjoyed each other. There was a lot of give and take between the two. Both of them reveled in their verbal sparring sessions. So, after Bo had growled at Jim that he had better be ready when the time came, Betts responded behind a sly grin, "Don't worry; anybody can go in there and hand the ball off." Betts breaks up with a laugh when thinking about it today.

For his part, Bo was equal to the moment. He knew that Betts should be playing somewhere. He wasn't going to fight it, and after Betts made the remark about handing the ball off, Bo's only response was, "Go on, and get the hell out of here."

His teammates, and I'm proud to include myself in that group, call Jim Betts, "Rope." We all got nicknames at some point, and "Rope" is what I've called him for over 30 years. He also knew what he was doing when he moved himself over to the defense.

In his senior year, "Rope" started next to Thom Darden at safety and became one of the best defensive backs in the conference. It was remarkable, since it was his first year playing the position. In one game he graded out from the coach's film at a perfect 100 percent. He didn't miss an assignment, and he made every play he could possibly have made in that game. Believe me when I tell you, the coaches were tough when they graded film. A perfect game was unheard of, but "Rope" pulled it off.

By the way, Betts also played a few series at quarterback that season. Bo was just keeping him ready.

Facial Hair

The late 1960s and early 1970s were turbulent times in this country. An unpopular war raged half a world away. College campuses were becoming centers for antigovernment student protests. The University of Michigan was not immune from these activities. There were Students for Democratic Society offices just off campus. Civil rights issues and protests actually closed classes on occasion. Women burned their bras on the Diag, and tie-dyed T-shirts were the wardrobe of the day in Ann Arbor.

Into all of this came Bo Schembechler in 1969. He was, and still is, conservative with a capital "C." It was his way or the highway. For Bo, there was right, and there was wrong. There was black, and there was white, and there was no gray area in any issue. Bo's arrival on the scene was a little like oil and water trying to coexist.

As football players for Bo and students at Michigan, we found ourselves caught between two worlds. During the day in class, we had all of the political and social issues of the day to deal with, and in the afternoon at football practice, we had a disciplined, no-nonsense leader who was tough, and demanding, and didn't accept any excuses. We learned from him the importance of teamwork. We were successful doing it his way.

Up on campus, individual expression was the norm. That didn't jive with what we learned would work in Michigan Stadium. The team, the team, the team, was the gospel according to Bo.

As I look back on it, I can tell you that all of us who played football during that tumultuous time were very lucky. We grew and experienced life on campus but had a man who was our anchor down at the Stadium. We couldn't get too carried away with the times, because we all were grounded to certain values by Bo.

We are all better off today for his presence and leadership during that time. If you ask those who played for him, it's my bet they'll all agree.

When the two worlds collided, it got pretty interesting. Bo had to come to grips with some issues that he couldn't just ignore, and he did. It was during this time that Bo also let a player get the best of him, for maybe the first and last time.

The player was Jim Betts. It just so happened that Bo's standard for personal appearance was a little different than the standard for the day. He did not like mutton-chop sideburns, long hair, or facial hair. He made it clear that on his team, these looks were not acceptable. Most of us figured, well, that's it. We won't look "cool" or "groovy" like some of the other guys on campus.

That was the prevailing attitude, except for Betts. He was a smooth talker, and he was sure he could fix this up with Bo. He also knew it wouldn't be easy, but he was going to try. As "Rope" says today, "That may have been one of my all time great maneuvers."

When Bo had the meeting with us and declared everything except the black players' afros off limits, Betts says, "That was really messed up. I'm just getting to where I can *see* my mustache, and he

Jim Betts shows off his facial hair and afro.

wants me to shave it off. I wasn't going for it, but I knew I better have a pretty convincing argument."

Jim thought about his approach to Bo on the subject, formulated his plan, and showed up at Bo's office the next day. "I understand the whole team concept you are espousing," Betts opened with, "and I understand how it's important that we don't have distractions that would interfere with the team concept. And I also want you to understand that the guys on this team are willing to do anything we have to do to be winners. But you stepped into an area that's pretty sensitive right about now."

At this point, Betts knew he had Bo's attention, so he charged ahead. "This whole identity thing, as it relates to a black man's heritage, is the issue. You've asked that we shave off our mustaches, which is basically denying who were are as people. I find that difficult to do at this time of my life. If you look around," Betts rolled on, "you won't see a black man without a mustache. After all the things we've been through as it relates to slavery and things that followed, there are certain things we're able to hold on to that differentiate us from anybody else, and having a mustache is one of those things."

"Rope" starts to smile as he remembers what happened next in this meeting with Bo. "He looked at me," Jim chuckles "and Schembechler said, 'What kind of happy horseshit is that?'"

Somehow, Betts kept a straight face, and told Bo he was serious. "I remember telling him about an incident in Washington where some guys were asked to sign a letter of loyalty," Jim continued, "and that kind of thing will divide a team rather than bring it together. I think it's gonna cause a problem, and I feel strongly about it. I'll do anything else, but I won't shave my mustache.

"He looked at me real funny-like. He wasn't sure! He just did not know how to take it! He wasn't sure whether I was serious," Betts grins. "And it was the first time I had a hard time keeping myself from laughing. I should have been laughing through the whole thing!" Jim says today. "But I maintained my serious look. As a matter of fact, I should have been up for an Academy Award for that performance!" Betts says with great pride.

Betts says that Bo dismissed him without saying anything other than, "Get the hell out of my office." But the next day, Betts learned his plan had worked. "When we got in the circle around Bo for the next day's workout," Betts recalls, "He said, 'I've been informed that it's a black man's heritage to have a mustache. So the black guys can keep theirs, but you white guys don't have that heritage, so I don't want to see that crap on your faces.'"

Betts says he was shocked! "I never thought he was going to buy it! I was prepared to shave mine off! Since he did buy it, though, I thought, 'I'll just keep mine.'" Betts says, chuckling.

"Rope" remembers only one player who suspected there were some shenanigans afoot. "Henry Hill looked at me and smiled, but I played dumb, like I had no idea what had gone on," Betts laughed.

"It Was Obvious!"

The Michigan vs. Michigan State football game has created some great finishes over the years. It shouldn't surprise anyone that these two teams find a way to give their best effort when facing off. Bitter rivals from the same state, you pull out all the stops. Sometimes things don't end the way one side thinks they should have ended. The cry of "We wuz robbed!" seems to be heard more in this game than in others. In recent history, it's gotten even more pronounced.

Take, for example, the game in 2000. Michigan's Larry Foote recovers a key Spartan fumble late in the game that looked like it should have been ruled out of bounds. "We wuz robbed!" cried the Michigan State faithful as they left Michigan Stadium.

Take, for example, the game in 2001. The MSU clock operator stops the clock with one second remaining when it appeared to everyone in Spartan Stadium that the clock should have run out and the game should have been over, delivering a Wolverine victory. The Spartans use the extra second to throw a TD pass and beat Michigan, despite an obvious holding penalty that was not called by an official. "We wuz robbed!" cried the Michigan faithful as they left Spartan Stadium.

Back in 1990, there was another controversial finish to this classic, and if you talk to Michigan fans, it is a day that will live in infamy. The Wolverines had been trailing Michigan State most of the game. They put on a furious comeback and scored a touchdown in the final moments to make it a 28-27 score in favor of the Spartans. Gary Moeller was in his first season as Michigan's head coach, and he decided to roll the dice and go for the two-point conversion.

As the Wolverines lined up for the play, Michigan quarterback Elvis Grbac saw his lightning-quick wide receiver, Desmond Howard, in man-to-man coverage against the Spartans' Eddie Brown. Grbac changed the play at the line and checked into a pass play to Desmond. Howard made a great fake to the outside and busted back inside. He had Brown beaten. Grbac threw the ball, and while the pass was floating in to Desmond for the Michigan win, Brown tackled him. As Howard was falling down from the interference, the ball hit him in the chest, but it bounced incomplete when Desmond hit the ground. *There was no flag on the play!*

Well, the boo-birds came out with full volume. Michigan Stadium was in an uproar. Gary Moeller was halfway to the end zone protesting. There would be no justice on this one. Michigan State held on for the 28-27 win.

Howard, the man in the middle of this controversy, says there was no question in his mind what had happened. "I definitely thought there would be a flag," says Desmond. "When you are playing at home and you know what is at stake and it boils down to that play, I assumed that the referees would have their attention on the field and on the skilled position players who were involved in that play. To me, it was obvious. I don't know how he could have missed it."

Today, after a solid NFL career and a Super Bowl MVP trophy, Howard is a bit more philosophical than some of the more rabid Michigan fans. "You know, everybody has a job to do," Desmond continues. "I just told everybody after the game that it wasn't my fault that the referee missed the call. It's obvious what Brown did, but the referee missed it. I had to move on."

Coach Gary "Mo" Moeller didn't like the call.

Desmond says he has never met Eddie Brown to talk about the now infamous interference that wasn't called that day, but he has heard stories. "I've seen quotes from him where he said he did what he had to do. And really," Desmond chuckles, "I can't blame him. If I was a defensive back and was beaten on the play that was going to decide the game, I probably would have grabbed and tripped the guy, too. So, I guess he admitted to it. I mean, there's so much evidence, it's hard not to."

The point that most people miss in this whole scenario is that Michigan did not win or lose because of the missed call. All the Wolverines wanted was the call to be made so that they could place the ball on the one-yard line and get another shot at the two-point conversion. There is no guarantee that they would have made it. The real shame of the non-call was that Michigan never got the chance. The game goes down in history as a 28-27 MSU win.

"His Face Was Right on My Shoulder!"

Another unbelievable moment at Michigan Stadium involving referees and an interference call occurred in November 1971. This particular call, though, went Michigan's way, and I was right in the middle of it.

The Wolverines were battling Ohio State. Michigan entered the game with a perfect 10-0 record, while Ohio State did not have one of their better teams. Nonetheless, Woody Hayes had his team primed and ready, despite the fact that they were big underdogs. It was a tight defensive struggle. Michigan led 3-0 on a Dana Coin field goal until Ohio State's Tom Campana returned a punt for a touchdown, and the Buckeyes carried a 7-3 lead late into the fourth quarter.

With about six minutes to play, Michigan finally mounted a drive. Larry Cipa was in at quarterback, and he was great. We moved the ball down the field for a go-ahead score. When Billy Taylor roared into the end zone on a power sweep around right end, we had finally taken the lead 10-7, with just about two minutes left in the game.

As Ohio State took over, they mounted a drive to either win or tie the game. They were fighting the clock and the Michigan Stadium crowd, but they moved the ball on us. We weren't out of the woods yet. With about a minute to play, the Buckeye quarterback went back to pass and fired a laser down the middle of the field to his tight end. Thom Darden, the Michigan safety, leaped over the tight end and made a great interception to seal the victory. There was contact between Darden and the Ohio State player, but it was a remarkably athletic play and a good interception. Darden had put it away. We were unbeaten with an 11-0 record.

We were celebrating like you couldn't imagine, until we noticed that Coach Hayes was in the middle of the celebration. He was 25 yards onto the field, and he wasn't celebrating. He was steaming mad!

Hayes thought that Darden interfered with *his* receiver. He had charged from the sideline to the middle of the field!

Jerry Markbreit was the referee for that game. Markbreit is a highly respected official who spent nearly 50 years officiating football. He worked Big Ten and Mid-American conference games early in his career before moving on to the NFL. He was chosen to work Super Bowls, which is a prized NFL assignment. For Markbreit, though, nothing he experienced in his entire career came remotely close to his confrontation with Woody Hayes that Saturday in Michigan Stadium.

"I was the referee, lined up behind the offense," Markbreit remembers. "So I'm about 40 yards away from the play. When the play was over, I looked down the field and saw one of my deep officials signaling the ball going over to Michigan. So I know it's an interception. I come all the way downfield. I stand over the ball and indicate that it's Michigan's ball, and I'm about to give the 'ready for play' signal, when I look over my shoulder and there, about 40 yards onto the field, is Woody! I reach into my pocket, grab my flag, fire it up in the air, turn to the press box, and signal unsportsmanlike conduct. Woody's face was right on my shoulder!

"He must have followed me around for five minutes," Markbreit recalls. "He was screaming and yelling. He called me everything you can imagine. He called me a pipsqueak. He called me a shit-heel. Woody screamed at me, 'You're going to change this call! You're the head of this crew. You're going to turn it around! That was interference and you know it!'"

Markbreit says he remained cool despite Coach Hayes's verbal assault. "Because we were close to the Michigan sideline," Markbreit recalls, "the security guy from Michigan stepped out on the field and asked me if I needed any help getting Woody off of me. I told him to just leave it alone. Finally, the Ohio State assistant coaches came out and dragged him off the field."

It wasn't over yet, remembers Markbreit. "When he gets to the sideline, he really starts going crazy, screaming and yelling, but we continue the game. On the next play, an Ohio State player comes in and smashes the Michigan center with a forearm to the face, right in front of me, so I flag that, and it comes with an automatic ejection in college ball. Now, the referee, when he ejects someone, has to walk the player to the sideline."

Markbreit says when he started his walk to the sideline, he was taken aback again. "When I looked to the Ohio State bench, I saw Woody breaking the down markers and kicking the chain crew! When I saw that, I turned to the Ohio State player and said, 'You're going to have to walk yourself over to the sideline. I don't want to go over there. Coach Hayes will probably kill me if I go over there,'" Markbreit remembers with a chuckle.

Markbreit says nothing matched that experience for the rest of his career. He also said it was a tremendous experience and great training for his NFL career. Markbreit figured he had seen the worst, so he could handle anything.

While Hayes was wreaking havoc on his sideline, Bo Schembechler was standing on the Michigan sideline taking it all in. Woody's performance was a classic moment at Michigan Stadium, but Bo also knew Woody well enough to know that the old coach didn't do anything without a plan behind it. "Woody's glasses were all steamed up," Bo recalls with a smile, "so I know he couldn't see. I just felt as I watched him out there, something else was going on. I said to myself, 'Woody, you know this game is gone. It's in the loss column.' You know what he was doing?" Bo asked rhetorically, "He was getting ready early, for next year. That's exactly what he was doing!" Bo concluded emphatically.

"He Back-to-Backed Me!"

During Bo Schembechler's years, he had occasion to question an official emphatically at times. Bo will tell you it wasn't as much as has been reported, but there was one instance when Bo got penalized twice on the same play.

Normally, coaches don't get penalties, but on this occasion, an unusual circumstance led to a great tale from Michigan Stadium.

The Wolverines were playing Texas A&M. During that period, when teams from different conferences met, the officiating crew would be evenly divided between the two conferences. They called it a *split crew*. If Michigan was playing a Pacific-10 team, half of the officials came from the Pac-10, and half came from the Big Ten. It was a system that the powers in college football felt would create a nonbiased look from the officials' standpoint at an interconference game.

Nowadays, when that situation occurs, an officiating crew from a neutral conference is assigned to the game. But for that Texas A&M game in 1977, half of the officials came from the Southwest Conference and half came from the Big Ten.

Both teams were nationally ranked in the top five. It was a big national matchup. Emotions were running high on both sides. As the game progressed, Michigan dominated the Aggies. As Bo told me recently, "Texas A&M had that Wishbone team with the big fullback, George Woodard, and we kicked their ass." Bo rarely forgets the good ones, and he's right about this one. Michigan wound up winning the game 41-3. But it wasn't without a hysterical moment that revolved around the split officiating crew.

Bo was prowling the sidelines during the game as he usually did, barking at his players and coaches. He had a habit of barking extremely loudly at a player if he made a mistake or missed an assignment during a play. It was an amazing phenomenon that with over 100,000 people in the stands making noise, players could hear Bo over the din. Take it from me; I had it happen more than once. For some unknown reason, his voice pierced through the noise *from 30 or more yards away.* You knew exactly who it was, and you knew Bo wasn't happy.

On one occasion during the game with A&M, Bo saw something he didn't like, and he let the offending player know about it. He bellowed from the sideline so that the message would be clearly understood. The next thing you know, a penalty flag floated right down in front of the Michigan bench.

That made Bo even madder than he already was, so he asked the wing official in front of the Michigan bench, who, by the way, was from Texas, what the penalty was for and who it was on. The official told Bo it was on him and marched away.

Bo says he was stunned! "I really believe," Bo says, "that the reason I got the second penalty is because that official called the first penalty on me when I was yelling at a player. When he told me the penalty was on me, I said, 'Well, you rotten SOB!' So he marched off 15 more! *He back-to-backed me!"*

Bo laughs about it today, and to hear him tell the story will have you in tears of laughter. Bo still contends, though, that he was justified. "I did not deserve the first penalty! That's why I was so mad," Bo remembers. "I don't even know what I said to the player, but this official must have been moving in toward the ball from our sideline and heard me. He must have thought I was yelling at him, so he turned around and threw the flag on me. When he told me the flag was on me, I got really hot! So he marched off another one. I cost us 30 yards!" laughed Bo.

There Would Be a Knock at the Door

As a team goes through a football season, they play a certain number of away games and a certain number of home games. So Michigan Stadium, to a degree, could be considered "home" for thousands of players and millions of fans over the years. But imagine if it really was your home. What if you really lived there? For Pat Hatch, that was exactly the case.

There was a time when a house sat outside the Stadium walls but inside the fence at the south end of Michigan Stadium. It was the home of longtime equipment manager Henry Hatch. Pat Hatch was his daughter, and from 1952 to 1964 Pat Hatch did indeed call Michigan Stadium her home.

Her memories of those years are vivid, but I quickly learned that football games didn't dominate her thoughts about living in a home with Michigan Stadium as a backyard. After all, the Stadium is used for football only seven or eight times a year. Pat Hatch lived there for 365 days a year.

"One thing that stood out in my mind," Pat told me, "was standing at the south end of the Stadium and watching President Lyndon Johnson give the commencement speech in 1964."

The house at the bottom left of the Stadium was the home of Pat Hatch.

As Pat talked, I realized her recollections of the Stadium are far different from most of ours. We all think of our experiences as part of an event. She thinks of her experiences at Michigan Stadium as part of everyday life. "I can remember on Saturdays after games," Pat says, "my dad would have to take care of his duties with the equipment. After he got home from that, my mother and dad and I, as a family, would walk around and check all the gates to make sure that they were locked."

Pat also said there was an occasion or two when unlocking the gates at the Stadium was part of the family's duties. "On most nights, we would lock the gates around 10 or so. Several times, I remember, there would be a knock at our door after 10 at night. There would be a couple standing at our door who had been sitting in the Stadium. They had stayed too late, and they got locked in. So we would have to go let them back out. That was kind of interesting," Pat says with a hint of laughter.

There were certain perks that came along with the house. The Hatches had the best parking you could imagine for game days. "We had a parking spot inside the fence right next to one of the restrooms," Pat remembers. "And I got to ride my bike all around the Stadium and never had to worry about traffic or anything.

"Game days were hectic, though," Pat says. "There was a gentleman from Chicago who got to know my mother because she worked at the ticket office. He bought all of his tickets through her. He would always stop at our house before a game and drop off his briefcase at the front door and pick it up after the game.

"It was fun to sit there on our porch before a game and watch the crowd build," Pat recalls. "Then I could just walk out my back door and over to my seat.

"I had a dear, sweet grandmother who would watch the games with me," Pat says. "My mother and father were working, so she would go with me to watch the games. Even though she couldn't see very well, those were her boys down on the field, and she would cheer for Michigan."

Pat says that even though they lived at the Stadium and had great parking, they still had to buy their tickets for the games like everyone else.

Like her grandmother, Pat Hatch still cheers for Michigan. She goes to every game she can. She doesn't live at the Stadium anymore, but she remembers the days when she would walk into the Stadium at night all by herself and reminisce. "It was really special!"

"I Thought the World of Him"

The relationship between Bo Schembechler and Woody Hayes is well-documented. After Michigan upset Ohio State in 1969 in Bo's first year as the Wolverine coach, the media seemed to focus on their relationship. Part of the reason was because Coach Hayes was such a huge figure in collegiate football. When one of his former assistants beat one of Woody's greatest teams in a huge upset, their relationship took on a life of its own. As a matter of fact, Woody once told Bo about that 1969 game, "You'll never win a bigger game."

It began the Woody vs. Bo era. For 10 years they met every November, leading their teams into a game that, in most cases, decided the Big Ten title and Rose Bowl berth. While the following story doesn't happen in Michigan Stadium, it is still a very good tale about a coach who was the archenemy to the Wolverines for many years.

The competition between Bo and Woody wasn't just on the field. After the 1969 game, it moved to the homes of high school prospects in recruiting. Bo had great success in recruiting the state of Ohio, and Woody didn't like that too much. Schembechler tells the story that Woody used to follow him wherever he went on the recruiting trail. "I would go in to talk to an Ohio prospect," Bo says, "and when I was about to leave, I would tell the young man, 'Now listen, tomorrow, Coach Hayes will be here, and he'll want to talk to you about Ohio State.' The prospect would tell me that Woody wasn't scheduled in to see him. He would say, 'Coach Hayes was in about a week ago, he's not coming tomorrow.' I would say, 'Trust me, Coach Hayes will be here tomorrow.'" Sure enough, Bo remembers, "Woody would come marching in to this kid's high school the next day. It was like he had spies around or something," Bo laughs.

Such is the case with Rob Lytle.

Lytle was a great young running back out of Fremont, Ohio. He was being recruited by all the major football powers from USC to Notre Dame. Bo had worked on Lytle very hard, though, and had gotten him to commit to Michigan. Lytle thought that was the end of the recruiting battle, but Coach Hayes wasn't done yet.

"Just before the signing date," Lytle recalls, "Coach Hayes drove up to Fremont because he said he wanted one more shot at me. He made me look him in the face and tell him I was going to Michigan. When I told him, he said, '*Why?*' With all my courage, I looked him in the eye and said I was going to Michigan because I thought it was a better fit for me." Lytle says Woody was not happy. "Coach Hayes growled at me and got up and left. He never shook my hand. He said, among other things, 'OK, we'll get along fine without you.'"

Lytle says Woody never spoke to him again. It doesn't sound like a very pleasant story, but it isn't over. The finish will surprise you. It gives an insight into Coach Hayes's character that isn't often revealed.

Lytle went on to a brilliant All-America career at Michigan. He was drafted in the early rounds of the NFL draft by the Denver Broncos. He had a solid career with Denver and the recruiting battle with Coach Hayes was long forgotten.

But Woody kept tabs on Lytle all through his NFL career. A teammate of Lytle's in Denver was Randy Gradishar. He had been a great linebacker at Ohio State, and Coach Hayes kept in touch with Gradishar by sending him notes through the mail. "Gradishar would come to me during the season and pass along these notes from Woody," Lytle says. "Gradishar would tell me, 'It's from Woody, and it's for you!' I mean, I was amazed!" Lytle exclaims.

According to Rob, the notes were very pleasant. They were encouraging. Coach Hayes would write Lytle to keep up the good work, and things like that. It was quite a turnaround from the last time they had seen each other, but Lytle says they still never talked, that he just got the notes.

Near the end of Lytle's playing career in the NFL, Woody surprised him one more time. "It was my fifth year, I think," Lytle remembers, "and I'd had about six surgeries on my knees and shoulders and I was about done. The year before, I had been way down on the depth chart. Red Miller was the coach, and he told me they would spot me on playing time. If another running back went down, I'd get some playing time, but it didn't look good," recalls Lytle. "About six games into the season, three running backs went down, bang, bang, bang. Well, I got in and had a great year. I got to play my natural position, and after the season, the coaches apologized for using me improperly. They told me I was in their plans to be more of a featured back. I should get ready for that role in the offseason."

Lytle says he felt as if his career had been renewed. Then the Broncos got sold. The entire coaching staff got fired while Lytle was on vacation. "Dan Reeves was hired as the coach," remembers Lytle. "I knew he was going to clean house. They had traded for a young running back out of Kansas City, which wasn't a good sign for me. So I figured I was done, again."

Still, Lytle was on the team, so he headed to training camp, and he was pitted against all the new young backs. "I had to prove my speed," Lytle recalls. "I had to prove that I was healthy, and I did, but I still wasn't sure I was going to make the team.

"Well, I made the last cut," Lytle says with relief, "and we were in a meeting before our first practice before the first regular-season game. Reeves was late for the meeting. We were all waiting for him, but he was really late. So another coach came in and started the meeting without Reeves. Finally, Reeves came in about the time we were finishing up, and he called my name out to see him.

"I figured I had either been traded or they were releasing me because they'd picked up somebody else," Lytle recalls. "So I went up there, handed my playbook to Reeves, and I went on the offensive. I said, 'At least you could have told me beforehand, before I got taped and dressed and all this crap.' Reeves looked at me and said, 'What the hell are you talking about?'

"'I'm sure I'm getting released or traded or something,' I said. 'Oh, hell no, you made the team before training camp started,' he said in surprise. Then he asked me a question that seemed odd. 'Didn't you play for Michigan?'"

Lytle says he told Reeves that he had. According to Lytle, Reeves then got a curious look on his face and said, "The reason I was late for the meeting is that Woody Hayes called me and wouldn't let me get off the phone."

Rob says he was shocked.

"Woody has been on my ass for 40 minutes," Lytle remembers Reeves saying. "I finally had to tell him I had players waiting for me and I was late for a meeting."

Lytle then asked Reeves what in the world Coach Hayes had called about. "You've got one of the biggest fans a guy could ever ask for," Reeves related to Lytle. "Coach Hayes called to tell me that the previous coach at Denver had made a huge mistake. Woody said they hadn't used you properly."

Lytle says Reeves couldn't get Woody off the phone! "He told Reeves I could do this, I could do that. I mean he built me up like I was the second coming of Christ," Lytle recalls with a chuckle.

Reeves finally said, "Coach Hayes told me I'd be nuts if I didn't play you regularly," according to Lytle.

Lytle says the whole episode took him by complete surprise.

Rob finally asked Reeves if Woody's call had helped, "I told Woody that you'd already made the team, and Woody said, 'Good, then you've made the right decision!'" Lytle remembers that Reeves was smiling as he finished the story.

Think about that. A full 10 years after Lytle and Hayes had last spoken, Woody was trying to use his influence to keep Rob's football career alive. For Lytle, it was an unbelievable gesture. After all, Rob had turned Woody down at Ohio State and gone to Michigan, Woody's archenemy. Yet Coach Hayes had kept an eye on his career the entire time. He had been in Lytle's corner all the way.

Say what you will about Woody Hayes, but he was a complex guy with some wonderful qualities. Many young men benefited greatly from their relationships with him, including a Michigan Wolverine named Rob Lytle, "He was very complimentary to me. I thought the world of him. I liked Woody."

"You Call Me Back in 24 Hours"

Recruiting is the lifeblood of a college coach. If you can recruit well, in most instances, you'll have a good team. Good players make good coaches. It is also a dog-eat-dog world out there in recruiting. Hundreds of schools will converge on the best high school athletes to try to convince them to enroll in this school or that school. All of the schools are after that special player.

This story is about Bo Schembechler's recruiting prowess. Michigan Stadium gets filled every week because the program wins. The players provide great theater for the Wolverine faithful. Schembechler was one of the best at bringing in the best and molding them into a team. This is a story about one who got away. It is a story about a coach who didn't sacrifice his integrity in the recruiting wars.

Fritz Seyferth was the recruiting coordinator at Michigan in the mid-1980s. "We had not been very successful recruiting the state of California, and we were on the top running back in California,"

Fritz began. "Cam Cameron had California as his recruiting area at the time, and he called the offices one night. It had to be at 11 at night or midnight. Cam told us that he had the best running back in the state with him, and this young man was ready to commit to Bo and agree to attend the University of Michigan."

This young man had also been recruited heavily by Colorado. Former Michigan assistant coach Bill McCartney was the head coach at Colorado at the time, and he and Bo were friends. They talked frequently.

"So Bo told Cam to put the young man on the phone," Fritz continued. "When he got on the phone, Bo said, 'So you want to come to Michigan?' The young man responded that he did, and Bo then said, 'Well, it's my understanding that you told Coach McCartney two days ago that you were going to Colorado. It seems to me son, that you've made a commitment to one coach already. I'll tell you what I want you to do for me,'" Seyferth remembers Bo saying, "'You call me back in 24 hours, and if you have not made a commitment to Coach McCartney, I'll accept your commitment to Michigan. But, if you've made a commitment to Coach McCartney, you are going to Colorado.'"

Fritz says he could almost hear Cameron on the other end of the line fall on the floor. "This just wasn't any player," Fritz says, "It was the top player in California!"

The next day, the young prospect called Bo and apologized. He said he had indeed committed to Colorado, and he was going to play for Coach McCartney.

I'm not sure if there is a moral to the story, but clearly, Bo taught everyone involved a lesson. From Fritz, to Cam, to the young prospect, everyone understood that Bo Schembechler was going to do it the right way. Even if it cost him an outstanding recruit, Bo wouldn't compromise his standards. His integrity intact, Schembechler never strayed from doing it the right way, on the recruiting trail, or in Michigan Stadium.

He Paid Me out of His Own Pocket

Back in the days of Yost, there was no recruiting. Players came from all over the country to go to school. They played football because they wanted to. There were no full-ride scholarships, and it wasn't an easy road.

Hercules Renda came to Michigan in the mid-1930s from West Virginia. He had worked in the coal mines to earn the money he needed to attend Michigan. When he decided to go out for the football team, Harry Kipke was his coach. "I had $155 in my pocket when I came to Michigan," remembers Renda. "In the first week I had to pay tuition, which was $75 for out-of-state students. Then I had to buy books and pay fees, so it wasn't too long before I was broke."

As a coach, Kipke understood that Renda was a fine player. He could help Michigan football, so Kipke decided to lend a hand to his struggling halfback.

"Kipke was building a home between Ann Arbor and Ypsilanti on Geddes Road," Renda recalls, "and I was able to help clean up and baby-sit for his two kids. He paid me for that out of his own pocket. I wouldn't have been able to enroll for the second semester had it not been for Coach Kipke."

In today's world of collegiate athletics that probably would be a violation of NCAA rules, but in those days, it was a wonderful gesture by a coach helping one of his young players.

Kipke was also a whale of a coach, according to Renda. "He was different from Crisler," Renda told me emphatically. "He would kid with you on occasion. Crisler was all business, all the time. Kipke was just a regular guy, very easy to get along with."

Kipke also wasn't the type to tip his hand. Renda remembers the opening game in 1937 against Michigan State at Michigan Stadium. It was Kipke's last year before relinquishing the reins of the program to Crisler. "Before the game," Renda remembers, "I was out there fielding punts. It was my sophomore year, my first game on the varsity, because freshman didn't play on the varsity back then. Anyway, I must have dropped the first five punts that I tried to catch.

Harry Kipke

Hercules Renda

"Now, the starting lineup had not been announced yet," Renda continues, "so after warming up, we head back to the locker room. Kipke is announcing the starting lineup, and I'm thinking to myself, if he watched me try to catch those punts, I don't have a chance to start! But, as it turned out, he put me in the starting lineup."

Renda was a small man, even in those days, but starting that first game, thanks to Coach Kipke, was a huge thrill. The only problem for Renda turned out to be the game. On the first kickoff, Renda got kneed in the stomach and had the breath knocked out of him. On the next play the same thing happened. He could hardly continue, he says, but stayed out there, playing both offense and defense.

After Michigan had forced the Spartans to punt, Renda went back to field the ball. It was over his head, but he managed to snag it cleanly on a bounce. He immediately got snowed under by a host of Michigan State players. "That was my introduction to collegiate football!" Renda laughed.

A rough start, but if you ask Hercules Renda, he would do it again in a heartbeat.

Don't Be the Favorite

It is very difficult to win the Heisman Trophy. You have to be very good. You have to be lucky, to a degree. And, maybe more importantly, you shouldn't be the favorite for the award at the beginning of the season.

The Heisman is a publicity-friendly award. If you want to get in the running, a lot of universities with bonafide candidates will put their media relations departments to work. I've seen fliers from schools that tout the statistics and accomplishments of certain players pushing them for the Heisman. They are professionally produced, full-color brochures, selling a youngster. In the 2001 season, a school from out West actually bought a billboard in Times Square in New York. It was a bigger-than-life full-length image of their quarterback.

At Michigan, that kind of thing has never been the practice. It may stem back to the Schembechler era when he just refused to promote an individual for an award. Bo always felt the team was more important, and if a team was successful, an individual would reap the rewards he justly deserved, playing within the team concept.

So in a way, it is odd that in the decade of the 1990s, two Wolverines were awarded college football's highest individual honor. Desmond Howard and Charles Woodson both won the Heisman. Before those two, only Tom Harmon had won the trophy in all the years of Michigan football. The media relations department didn't push Howard or Woodson, so what was the difference in the 1990s?

For a theory, you go to Jim Schneider, the longtime media relations man at Michigan. Jim is usually behind his desk at Schembechler Hall under a mound of papers and memorabilia. His office is organized chaos. Only he knows where to find anything, but his theory on the Heisman is very clear. "The key is to *not* be the favorite," Schneider says. "You do not want to be the guy they focus on all summer. Neither Desmond nor Charles was the leading candidate going into the season. Desmond came on in the Boston College game with four touchdowns. And remember," Schneider goes on, "Derrick Alexander got hurt in that game, and he was a great receiver. With Derrick out, Desmond got a lot more catches than he might have. The two favorites that year were [David] Klinger, and [Ty] Detmer, and they both had terrible games early on. Then Desmond made The Catch against Notre Dame. He got everybody's attention, and each week after that, did something else."

Jim says that from a publicity department's perspective, everything worked for Desmond that year, even the World Series. "The one Saturday we didn't play was the week we were in Minnesota," Jim went on. "Because of the World Series in the Metrodome, our game with Minnesota was moved to a Friday night. We were the only team to play on Friday, so every media outlet in America had our highlights for their Saturday pregame shows. Desmond broke two records that night, and it just so happened that one of the records was Anthony Carter's. Wouldn't you know, Carter was in the stadium. He played for the Vikings then, but because it was a

Charles Woodson poses with his Heisman.

Friday night, he hadn't left for their road trip yet, so he was there to pass the torch to Desmond. It was all perfect timing!"

In Woodson's case, Schneider says the preseason favorite was Peyton Manning, and he very easily could have won the award. But, Schneider says, "Charles did something spectacular each week. He made a great interception against Michigan State. He ran for a touchdown against Minnesota. He then threw a pass to Griese in one game. He caught a touchdown pass against Penn State. And against Ohio State, he intercepted a pass, caught a pass, and returned a punt for a touchdown.

"Because neither of them was the favorite going into the season," Jim states, "the media didn't have a chance to chip away at them. In Manning's case, he had never beaten Florida, so they chipped away at him."

Jim says the chipping happened to a Michigan player in 1994. "Remember Tyrone Wheatley?" Schneider asks. "He had the great game against Washington in the Rose Bowl, and for six months he was a candidate. The next year they chipped away at him until he wasn't a candidate." Wheatley finished eighth in the Heisman voting that season.

It's all a matter of timing, talent, luck, and *not* being a candidate.

"It's an Umbrella!"

Michigan Stadium has seen some amazing turns in games. No game, though, had a more amazing turnaround than the 1981 contest between Michigan and Illinois.

The Illini came into the game with an explosive passing attack, and they dominated the Wolverines in the first quarter. It looked as though it was going to be a blowout win for Illinois. They had built a 21-7 lead, and the game wasn't 15 minutes old. To say the faithful at Michigan Stadium were in a state of shock was an understatement.

In the second quarter, the Illini were driving again in the Michigan red zone, looking to make it a 28-7 lead, when Wolverine defensive back Jerry Burgei intercepted a Tony Eason pass to thwart the Illinois scoring drive. It was the key play in the game, because Michigan, from that point on, destroyed Illinois.

The Wolverines scored 63 unanswered points and turned what looked like a sure defeat into a blowout Michigan win.

One of the plays that seemed to break Illinois completely in that game came just before the half. Longtime Michigan equipment man Jon Falk was on the sidelines for this play, and he remembers it vividly. "There wasn't much time left in the first half, I think under a minute," Falk recalls. "Our quarterback, Steve Smith, went back to pass. As he's going back, I hear Gary Moeller, our quarterbacks coach, scream from the sidelines, *'It's an umbrella, It's an umbrella!'* The Illinois defense was in a coverage where the defensive backs had shaded the left and right sidelines," Falk remembers. "They had left the middle of the field wide open! Smith must have heard Moeller, because Steve took off on a quarterback draw and went 42 yards up the middle for a touchdown."

If you remember the play, Smith went in untouched. He split the hash marks, and there wasn't an Illinois defender within 20 yards of him for the entire run. The touchdown made it a 28-21 Michigan lead at the half. They had come back from a 21-7 deficit, which was almost a 28-7 deficit, to take the lead.

"I'll never forget that as long as I live," says Falk. "The feeling those players had in the locker room at the half was unbelievable after coming back like we did."

It must have been a bit of sweet revenge for Moeller also. Gary had been let go as the Illinois head coach just two years earlier after a three-year run with the Illini. He had left Illinois in the middle of a five-year plan and was just beginning to get it turned around when he got sacked. He had returned to Michigan on Bo Schembechler's staff the year after his tenure ended at Illinois. So, to call that play, at such a key moment, was a bit of justice for "Mo."

Michigan continued to dominate the game in the second half. Ultimately the Wolverines won it 70-21.

The postmortem on this game was just as interesting as the game itself. There were some members of the media and some members of the Illinois contingent who wondered aloud whether Michigan had run up the score. The Illini-Wolverine relationship was a bit strained, because Bo had publicly been critical of Illinois after they had fired his good friend Moeller.

Schembechler, for his part, bristles at the insinuation that he ran it up. "Anybody who gets beat by 70 points is going to say you ran it up," Bo said. "But the truth of the matter is we were scoring with our third-stringers in there. Hell, we were scoring with our fourth-stringers. We were scoring with everybody late in that game!"

"You Look Bigger in White"

Sometimes it's a matter of being in the right place at the right time. Sometimes it's a mistake that turns out to work better than you could have imagined. Sometimes a player has a great game despite himself. This is a story of a player who had that kind of game, and it cost him his starting position.

It was 1964, and Michigan was playing Minnesota. The Wolverines were on their way to a Big Ten title and Rose Bowl victory.

The captain of that Michigan team was Jim Conley. He watched his teammate, Bill Laskey, have a great afternoon at the Gophers' expense. "Laskey had one of the most fantastic days a defensive end could have. I mean, he had three sacks. He had an interception. He did everything." Conley says.

"We played a wide tackle six," Conley continues, "where the end drops off on the wide side of the field. Anyway, Laskey ended up getting named the Midwest Lineman of the Week for his performance. However, the coaching staff for Minnesota was amazed, because Laskey was never where he was supposed to be!

"When our coaches graded the film," Conley laughs, "Laskey was out of position so often, he graded out so poorly, that he was dropped down to the second team! At the time," Conley goes on, "the second team wore white jerseys, and the first team wore blue jerseys at practice. I remember Billy feeling so good about being Midwest Lineman of the Week; he couldn't believe he was bumped to second team. That Monday at practice, Jocko Nelson, one of our coaches, walked by Laskey in his white jersey and said, 'Don't let it bother you, Billy. You look bigger in white.'" Conley concludes with a laugh.

"Apparently, the Minnesota game plan didn't account for Laskey not doing what he was supposed to do," chuckles Conley, "so Billy had a great day despite himself."

Bill Laskey wears the preferred blue jersey.

It Was Orchestrated by the Walk-Ons

As I got going on this collection one thing became clear to me when I interviewed players from the mid- and late 1970s. Without exception, a game that stands out in all of their memories is their matchup with Texas A&M in 1977.

Curtis Greer was an All-America defensive lineman for the Wolverines in that battle with the Aggies. A moment just prior to kickoff stands out for him as one of the defining moments in his Michigan career.

"All during the offseason, we knew we had Texas A&M on the schedule in Ann Arbor," Greer remembers. "There weren't many teams we played from the Southwest Conference, and they had a great team. We had a number of sophomores and juniors who were starting on defense, and even though we had a few games under our belts, we knew they were a ranked team, and if we didn't bring our best game to the table, it was going to be a long afternoon for us.

"The most memorable moment in that game, for me, anyway," Curtis continues, "was right after we came off the field, running up the tunnel. Your thoughts are concentrating on the game plan. But when we walked into the Michigan locker room, it was just on fire. There was a level of electricity that I had never felt before. And it was really orchestrated by many of the walk-ons and individuals who weren't going to have an opportunity to play that day. But they were certainly going to make their contribution to the Michigan tradition, and the football program, by supporting us.

"When we walked out on that field," Greer says nostalgically, "we knew we weren't just representing ourselves. We weren't just representing the Michigan defense. We were representing tradition. Those walk-ons made a big contribution that day to Michigan football."

Obviously the contribution was significant, because the Wolverines beat the Aggies 41-3. "We smoked them!" Greer says with a smile. "Ron Simpkins was a great linebacker for us from Detroit, and he had some verbal comments early on in that game for A&M's great fullback, George Woodard. We knew after Simpkins made his remarks that the game was on! Simpkins set the tempo for us."

Ron Simpkins blocks a punt against A&M in 1977.

Greer says that Woodard didn't respond to those verbal comments by Simpkins very much, "How could he?" Greer smiles, "There were always about five or six Michigan helmets all over him!"

Simpkins and Greer also made an adjustment in that game, on their own, that helped them to a great defensive effort. The Aggies ran a Wishbone attack, and it was formidable. The fullback was a 280-pound bruiser, and the halfbacks had speed to burn. All week long in practice, the Wolverines had schemed a plan to stop this triple threat, but in the game, Simpkins and Greer changed it without telling the coaches.

"Curtis and I were playing on the same side. All week long, we game planned that the inside linebacker would take the fullback on their triple option," Simpkins remembers. "And the defensive end would take the quarterback. Now, this fullback was like 300 pounds! He was a load! I was a lot smaller than he was, and Curt was more his size."

Simpkins says that on A&M's first possession they moved it just past midfield, and their great kicker hit a long field goal. "We got to the sideline," Simpkins recalls, "and we said, 'We can't let these guys get to the 50, or they're going to score!' The next time the defense went out, I got to Curt and said, 'Look, we're going to change this game plan. You take the fullback, and I'll take the quarterback.' I don't think they did a thing the rest of the game," Simpkins says with pride.

It was a great victory for Michigan. Simpkins and Greer along with their defensive teammates had been brilliant. After the game, defensive coordinator Bill McCartney came up to congratulate Simpkins and said, "We had a great plan, and you guys were great!" Simpkins remembers telling McCartney that he and Greer had made a subtle change to the plan. According to Ron, McCartney thought about it for a moment and said, "That's great, but you shouldn't do that without telling us."

Whether they told McCartney or not, it worked to perfection. It saved Simpkins a headache or two and stopped Texas A&M cold.

We Were from the City

One of the great recruiting jobs Bo and his staff accomplished came in the mid-1970s. It was about the time that Curtis Greer and Ron Simpkins came to Michigan. They were from the Detroit Public School league. There was a wealth of talent during this time, and Bo never missed getting the great players out of the PSL.

In the 1975 class, Greer, Tom Seabron, Harlan Huckleby, and Roosevelt Smith, all out of Detroit Cass Tech, were huge contributors during their years. It wasn't long after that the likes of Simpkins, Mike Harden, Ralph Clayton, and Stanley Edwards followed from other PSL schools.

These young men formed part of the nucleus for the real glory years. From 1976 through 1980, Michigan won four Big Ten championships in five years. Most of the talent on those teams came from Detroit and the state of Michigan.

Having that kind of familiarity also created a kind of swagger with the group. Curtis Greer remembers his high school coach saying "Guys, you can go anywhere in the country, but I can assure you if you don't go together, you're not going to win a damn thing." Greer says that kind of guidance was invaluable. It drove home the point that the team was more important than the individual. They were already a team when they arrived in Ann Arbor. They brought the swagger with them from Detroit.

Along with the swagger came attitude. This group talked as good a game as they played. Greer, who is as classy a guy as you'll find, says with a measured smile, "On occasion, we had an opportunity to express ourselves." They all came from the city. They all talked a little trash to each other. It was expected.

According to sources that shall remain nameless, Simpkins was exceptional at "expressing himself." So we come to a game against Minnesota in 1977. The Wolverines were ranked as the nation's No. 1 team. In a stunning upset, Michigan lost in Minneapolis 16-0.

One of the Gophers' stars in that game was running back Marion Barber. He was also from Detroit, but he had gotten away from Michigan. Barber had grown up with and played against a lot of the Michigan players in high school, so he was very familiar. Apparently, there was a considerable amount of talk passing back and forth in this particular game between Barber and his Wolverine friends.

Simpkins remembers the scenario very easily. "You know, we were from the city," Ron recalls. "We had played against each other for three years in high school. We were friends. We were talking back and forth. It wasn't anything bad!

"Anyway," Simpkins goes on, "they end up beating us, and in the article the next day in the paper, Barber is quoted as saying, 'That Ron Simpkins guy, he talked bad about me the whole football game.' I couldn't believe it," Ron laughs.

"From that point on," Ron says with a sense of sweet revenge, "Barber never made it through the first quarter against Michigan the next three years! He was not going to play a full game. Our battle cry was *'Hold him up!'* He never played a full game against Michigan the rest of his career."

Marion Barber had broken the code and told tales out of school. The Detroit connection in Ann Arbor made sure he paid the price. The swagger never left, even in defeat.

Harlan Huckleby was part of the PSL gang from Detroit.

"Clothesline the Guy!"

It isn't often that a head coach chases an assistant coach around the practice field. But things were a bit different in Ann Arbor when Bo Schembechler arrived, so as players, we weren't surprised by too much. This particular event, though, did manage to get our attention.

In Bo's first year, we had very physical, tough practices. Spring ball was a challenge. Every day we would hit. It was live, first-team offense against first-team defense for all—or part—of the day. If you didn't fasten your chinstrap, your helmet was coming off.

Dick Hunter came with Bo to Michigan from Miami of Ohio as a member of his staff and was coaching the defensive backfield. Like all the coaches, Hunter was after his defensive backs to play tough and punish receivers whenever they could. On this particular day during spring ball the linebackers and secondary were battling against the receivers in a pass scrimmage. The linemen weren't involved. Hunter remembers the drill clearly. "It was always competitive as hell!" Hunter recalls. "Bo was running the offense, and he had this play where he ran the tight ends under our linebackers. The quarterback would sprint out and throw back to the tight ends, and they were just kicking our butts with that play. Well, I got mad," Hunter says with a laugh. "So I told Mike Taylor, our linebacker, to bump the tight end. I told him to knock him down."

As the drill continued, Bo ran that play to the tight end again, and while Taylor had bumped him, Jim Mandich, the tight end, still caught the ball. Hunter says he got furious, "I went into the defensive huddle and I told Mike, 'The next time they run that tight end underneath you, I want you to clothesline the hell out of the guy!' So the next time they ran the play," Hunter chuckled, "Taylor absolutely took the guy's head off. It wasn't Mandich, but the poor guy went down hard, and Bo saw it.

"Bo came over and he just ripped Mike's ass," Hunter says. "Mike stood there and took it, then turned around and looked at me. He asked me what to do now, and I told him, 'Mike, you've got to teach these guys that this is your territory, not theirs!'"

The drill concluded, and the practice moved to a goal-line scrimmage. The linemen joined this portion of practice, so we were into a live scrimmage. Bo put the ball at the eight-yard line, and the offense had three downs to score. If the offense didn't score in three downs, Bo got hot. If the defense didn't hold, Jim Young, the defensive coordinator, and his defensive coaches got mad. As players, we couldn't win, but we were used to it by then.

Hunter says he had his defense ready for the tight end pass by the time the scrimmage started. "When Mandich tried to run that route, he would grab guys and push them, so I told my defensive guys to drop his ass! And my guys did!" Hunter says with pride.

Jim Mandich was an All-America player, and Bo wasn't sure he liked the defense taking liberties with him. "Bo saw it again," Hunter remembers with a laugh, "so he came over and started yelling like hell at me, and I yelled like hell at him. When he got close," Hunter says, "I took off running because I knew he was going to push me."

As an observer, I can tell you it was hysterical. Bo took off after Hunter, running and chasing and yelling the whole time. Hunter was faster, so he was clearly not going to get caught, and you could see Dick smiling, which made Bo even madder. After a moment or two of this, even Bo realized the humor in the scene. He came back to the offensive huddle with a half-smirk on his face, and practice continued.

As I recall, Dick Hunter got some pats on the back from a lot of players after practice. Vicariously, a lot of us enjoyed him getting the better of Bo, even if it was for just the moment. The two former coaches remain good friends today and laugh heartily about that day whenever they get together at our frequent reunions.

"You've Got to Make a Trade"

When young men come out of high school to play college ball, their best position isn't necessarily their best position. That sounds kind of odd, but it really isn't. A great running back out of high school may be better suited to play defensive back. A defensive back out of high school may flourish as a receiver in college. It isn't an exact science, but the key for coaches is finding the best position for each player so that they are able to maximize their abilities.

Take, for example, Tyrone Wheatley. Out of high school, Wheatley was an All-State quarterback. In college at Michigan, he became a better running back. This tale concerns a pair of players who made changes that paid big dividends.

Back in the early seventies, Randy Logan was a brilliant defensive back for the Wolverines, and Bo Rather was a big-play wide receiver. They didn't start out that way, though.

Dick Hunter had Rather as a defensive back. Logan, meanwhile, was playing wingback on offense. Hunter remembers that Jim Betts, a veteran on the team, came to him one day and said, "'Dick, somehow you've got to make a trade.' So I traded Bo Rather for Randy Logan. We sent Rather to offense, and I got Logan.

"Randy was fumbling the ball all the time on offense," Hunter recalls. "He just couldn't do anything right, and Bo was on him all the time. Bo Rather, as a defensive back, wouldn't hit anybody. He just wasn't tough enough. He just didn't want to be there. Bo wanted to play offense. So we made the trade.

"What a great move it was, too," Hunter goes on. "Logan became an All-America corner and went to Philadelphia in the NFL. Rather played great as a wide-out and went on to the NFL with the Chicago Bears. And the idea for the trade came from Betts!" Hunter laughs.

Randy Logan

Bo Rather

"I Think That Would Be Great!"

It wasn't very often that Bo Schembechler surprised a lot of people, but in the fall of 1979 he surprised quite a few folks with a change in the lineup in the Wolverines' finale against Ohio State.

All season long, B.J. Dickey and John Wangler had been sharing time at quarterback. They were No. 1 and No. 2 virtually all season. A young freshman named Rich Hewlett had worked his way into the third-string quarterback position. It wasn't until game five, though, that Hewlett even made the travel squad. The prospect of Hewlett playing a great deal was remote.

Hewlett remembers that about midseason, his prospects improved. "Dickey got hurt with a shoulder or something," Rich recalls. "So Wangler moved in as the starter, and I was backing up John. In our second-to-last game against Purdue, we fell way behind in the first half, and Don Nehlen, our quarterbacks coach, kept telling me to get warmed up, that I was going in. At halftime, they kept telling me to get ready. I was going in. But Wangs kind of caught fire in the second half and nearly brought us back to win it. We should have won it, but didn't."

As it turned out, Hewlett never played in that game. Rich says he and Wangler joke about it today. "I spent the whole game warming up and never played a down," laughs Hewlett. But it was clear that he had caught the attention of the coaches. He had also stayed under the radar and out of the prying attention of the media.

Hewlett says the following Monday was an interesting day. "I was called up to the full staff meeting room after practice," recalls Hewlett. "Nehlen and Bo came walking in together and sat down. Bo looked at me and basically said, 'Rich, we want to start you against Ohio State. What do you think about that?'" Hewlett chuckles as he remembers the moment. "Being young, naïve, probably overly confident, and maybe a little cocky, I said, 'I think that would be great!'"

Hewlett hadn't started all year. He was a third-stringer when the season started. Nehlen and Schembechler then asked more questions, "'Do you think you're ready? Will you be able to handle it?' I kept saying, 'Sure, no problem.'"

"They then told me they didn't really want to tell the team until the week played out," recalls Hewlett. "I think they wanted to see how I practiced before they made a final decision. So that week at practice I spent more time with the first unit and I had a good week. Finally on Thursday after practice, Bo announced to the team that he was going to start me at quarterback."

Rich had known this was all going to happen since Monday, but other than Bo and the staff, nobody else was let in on the plan. Bo didn't tell anybody outside the team until Saturday prior to the kickoff against Ohio State. As a matter of fact, staff members of the sports information department, who are supposed to know these things, didn't even know. Everybody kept the secret until Hewlett took the field with the offense on the opening possession.

"I'm sure 99 percent of the people, including Ohio State, had to be surprised by it," Hewlett says. "Bo felt that starting me would be a good change-up, and maybe throw a curve at Ohio State. I was more of an option quarterback than John [Wangler], and Bo felt we had a very good defense. We had turned the ball over a lot the week before, so Bo thought if we kept the offense a little more conservative and controlled the ball, our defense would keep us in the game."

As it turned out, Michigan lost the game to Ohio State 18-15. Hewlett started but didn't finish. He was outstanding in his first start under intense pressure, but in the second quarter, Hewlett was back to pass and got sacked. His foot got caught in the turf, and he tore ligaments in his ankle. His day was done.

Rich Hewlett wasn't such a secret after that. The next season, he started the Wolverines' first two games. He engineered a win over Northwestern in the opener. Against Notre Dame in the second game, he gave way to Wangler in the second half, and the Irish won in South Bend when Harry Oliver hit a 51-yard field goal as time expired. After that, Rich went to a backup position behind Wangler again. In his junior year, he moved to the defensive side of the ball and finished his career as a defensive back.

As he looks back on it, the ankle injury in that hectic first start was one of those large "what-ifs" for Hewlett. "On each play and each series, I was getting better, and more confident," recalls

Rich. "You know, the game was moving so fast at first. I felt like a sponge. I was absorbing everything around me. I kept getting more and more relaxed. I played a little tentatively early, not wanting to make a mistake. I felt like if we got to halftime and made a few adjustments, I could get out there in the second half, get into a little comfort zone, and get the job done. I just felt that it was too bad I got hurt, not that John [Wangler] and I still wouldn't have shared time, but if I didn't get hurt, I feel I still could have played and contributed."

Despite the injury, make no mistake, Rich contributed greatly to Michigan football. In addition, Rich's surprise start against Ohio State let him experience a real bond with his teammates. "The team really rallied behind me that week," Hewlett says with obvious affection, "I have very fond memories of those guys. They really stood behind me. I mean, John Wangler was their classmate, and here I was, a snot-nosed freshman, stepping on his toes. Curt Greer, Ron Simpkins, John Arbeznick, Kurt Becker, I mean these guys really stood behind me and supported me. It's something I'll never forget about my days at Michigan Stadium."

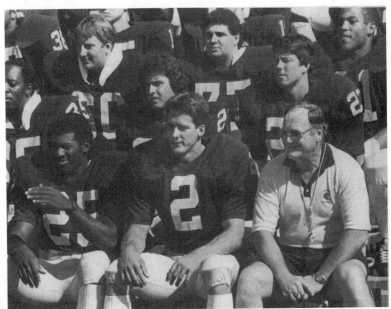

Rich Hewlett (No. 2) sits with Bo on picture day.

It Was a Magical Day

The last game in Michigan Stadium for the 1968 season was against Wisconsin. It was cold. It was raining. It was wet. The field was muddy, and the sledding was going to be tough. The official attendance for the game was only 51,117. For those fortunate 51,000 who showed up, they saw firsthand one of the greatest performances ever by a Michigan running back.

The Wolverines entered the game having won seven straight after an opening loss to California. Running back Ron Johnson was having a spectacular year, but he saved the best for his last appearance at The Big House. He ran over, around, and through the Badgers' defense for 347 yards on 31 carries that day. It was a record-shattering performance at the time. Michigan would go on to win easily 34-9, but for Johnson, his performance wasn't as pleasing to him as what had happened before the game.

"The president of the university, Robben Fleming," Johnson remembers, "invited my parents to sit up in his booth in the press box for that game. My parents had attended every game I played in at Michigan. Michigan Stadium was a great, great venue for us as a family, but they had always sat in the stands.

"For them to be in the press box, in that environment," Johnson recalls with pride, "was special. My father, who had a fourth grade education, and my mother, who had a 10th grade education, were overwhelmed. We were so proud of each other.

"They had past presidents, and all these people with eight-zillion degrees, coming up and shaking my father's and mother's hands. I felt so good for them to have that experience."

Ron laughs that it also wasn't such a bad thing that his parents were out of the inclement weather, either. "To have them in the press box and to have the kind of day I had was just perfect," Johnson says emotionally. "For me, it was a magical day."

Another amazing event in that Wisconsin game was that Johnson actually took himself out of the game! He could have had an even bigger day! "I remembered back to my sophomore year," Johnson says. "I was playing behind Carl Ward and Jim Detwiler, and they weren't bad. So, in my sophomore year, we were leading Minnesota big, and I finally got into the game in the fourth quarter. The first real playing time I got was great experience. You know, I was worried about fumbling and all that stuff when you first get the chance to play.

"So we've got the big lead against Wisconsin in my senior year, and I've had a great day," Johnson recalls. "My last play in that game was the first play of the fourth quarter. I went to Tony Mason, my coach, and told him to put Lance Sheffler into the game. Lannie was my backup. I told Tony to let the kid get some experience and have some fun, you know, that sort of thing.

"About five minutes later," Johnson says with a chuckle, "one of the statisticians came down to the field and asked me how many yards I thought I had. I told him that I thought I had around 200. He said, 'Ron, you've got 347 yards!' I mean, my mouth just dropped! I was dumbfounded!

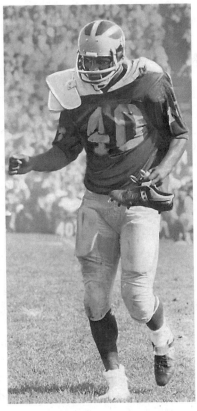

"Lannie went on to play well," Johnson says, "but I could have had maybe 400 yards that day. I was taken aback. I had no clue I had that many yards. I mean, the blocking was all so crisp. The holes were very defined and very easy to find. But we weren't about running up the score. The truth is," Johnson concludes, "the whole day, with my parents and my performance, just blew me away."

Ron Johnson (No. 40)
could have gotten even more.

"Let's Go Over to Colonial Lanes"

The year after Ron Johnson had his special day at Michigan Stadium, Bo Schembechler was hired to take over for Bump Elliott as Michigan's head coach. It is well documented that Don Canham, the athletic director at Michigan, took a chance on Schembechler. He wasn't a big name at the time, and it was a bold move. It was a little more bold than most of us originally had thought, based on a story told to me by one of Bo's assistants whom he brought with him to Michigan from Miami of Ohio.

Dick Hunter came to Ann Arbor with Bo from Miami. Hunter was the secondary coach, and along with Jim Young, Chuck Stobart, Gary Moeller, Jerry Hanlon, and Larry Smith, the transplants from Miami, they formed the nucleus of Bo's new staff. According to Hunter, Bo had to fight to bring them along.

"When Canham hired Schembechler," Hunter recalls, "Bo demanded that his six assistants were coming with him. I guess Canham resisted and told Bo that he had to hire some Michigan guys. I remember Bo coming back to Miami and telling us that he wasn't going unless he could take all six of us. Canham obviously gave in, and we all headed to Ann Arbor.

"We got up there early in January," Hunter says, "and about the end of the month, Canham came to the six of us from Miami, and said, 'C'mon, guys, let's go over to Colonial Lanes. I'll buy you a drink. I need to talk to you guys.'"

Colonial Lanes is a bowling alley just up the street from the athletic offices, and the bowling alley housed a tavern called the Pin Room. It was, and still is, a gathering place for some of the athletic department personnel. Rumor has it that it was a particularly favored place for Canham, and a great deal of business was conducted there. Now, don't tell anybody you heard that from me.

Anyway, Hunter says the six new assistants headed over to Colonial Lanes unsure of what Canham wanted, because Bo was not included in the meeting. "Canham told us," Hunter remembers with a laugh, "he didn't want to hire us. He told us that Bo had forced

Photo courtesy of Bentley Historical Museum, University of Michigan

The 1969 coaching staff's job security wasn't guaranteed.

his hand to hire us. He said, 'I've received so many calls, nasty calls, because I didn't hire any Michigan guys, and if you guys don't win, I'm going to have to fire your asses right away.'"

Hunter says it was kind of a matter-of-fact meeting. They continued having a few drinks and talking. According to Hunter it was a very pleasant time, but as they were about to leave, Canham repeated, "Remember what I told you guys!"

"I'm thinking, 'Holy Christ!'" Hunter says, "'What did we get ourselves into?'"

"Anyway," Hunter continues, "we went on to have a great year. We beat Ohio State, and Canham has laughed about that meeting ever since. He's said many times since then that hiring Bo was the smartest thing he ever did. The six of us think so, too."

"You've Got to Play Better Than You Know How"

In the glory years of Michigan football under Fritz Crisler in the mid-1940s, the Wolverines won two national titles. During the 1947 and 1948 seasons, Michigan won 19 straight games. In the 1947 season they outscored their opponents by a combined score of 394-53. It was the era of the "Mad Magicians" in Ann Arbor, and halfback Bob Chappuis from Toledo, Ohio, was the master magician.

Michigan Stadium has seen its share of illusions, but Fritz Crisler's offense with Chappuis at the helm was the star attraction during those years. Chappuis says if anybody should be called a magician, it should be Coach Crisler. "We played that single wing with the spinning fullback," Chappuis recalls, "and from what I have gathered over the years, our deception was so great in that offense that the term 'Mad Magicians' came out of it. Nobody could find the ball, including, sometimes, the coaches!" Chappuis laughs.

An offense like that doesn't just happen. There have to be great precision and hours of practice to pull it off, and Chappuis says Crisler's attention to detail as a coach was the main reason for success. "He was quite a taskmaster," Chappuis says, "a very, very austere guy, almost standoffish. He didn't get too close to the players. But he had the respect of us all. You know, I still have a tough time calling him 'Fritz.' We either called him 'Coach' or 'Mr. Crisler,' but never 'Fritz.'"

Chappuis says Coach Crisler was a master motivator. The "Mad Magicians" weren't loaded with super-talented guys according to Chappuis. "Coach Crisler's favorite line was, 'You've got to play better than you know how.'" Chappuis continues, "And we did that. I've said many times that we didn't have great football players. We had good football players, and we all knew one another and respected one another. This may sound like and old cliché, but we did have chemistry."

What an understatement! The Wolverines of 1947 were unbeaten and went to the Rose Bowl, where they clobbered Southern

California 49-0. It was preparation for that Rose Bowl that produced another story about Crisler's ability to motivate.

"We took the train to California," Chappuis recalls, "and it took us about three days to get there. We got there about three weeks ahead of time, and we went through several two-a-day practices. Well, two days before the game, we were running through plays before the end of a practice just to work up a sweat. And while I was running this one play I went down with a terrible pain in my leg. I didn't know exactly what had happened, but I had an idea that I had pulled a hamstring."

"I was on the ground, and really in pain," Chappuis remembers, "and Coach Crisler came over and looked down at me. He then looked at Jim Hunt, our trainer and said, 'Jim, what happened here?'

"Hunt said, 'Well, I think Bob has pulled his hamstring.' So Coach looked down at me and said, 'Good thing it didn't happen to somebody who could run!'" Chappuis laughs out loud as he relates the story. "I'll tell you, though," Chappuis goes on, "I never got up off the ground so fast in all my life."

Chappuis says that many years later, at a reunion of that team, the story came up again. "One of my teammates, Bruce Hilkene, told me that the team was kind of shook up when they saw me lying there on the ground," Chappuis says with a chuckle, "but Bruce said that when Mr. Crisler looked down at me and said what he did, it made them all feel a lot better. 'We knew we could get along without you,' Hilkene said."

Chappuis says that he realized then what Crisler was doing that day. "Coach Crisler wanted me to get off the ground, number one. And number two was that he wanted the players on the rest of the team to know that I wasn't the only guy there! He was so great with the way he said things. He spoke in sort of a monotone. He was very serious. You knew when he said something that he really knew what he was talking about."

Chappuis went on to play in the Rose Bowl and play very well. He broke two Rose Bowl records for total offense and pass completions.

Bob Chappuis is in action, no hamstring problems.

For the trip back to Ann Arbor on the train, Chappuis says he and his teammates got another treat. "We were all kind of partying and having a good time," Bob recalls, "and Coach Crisler came into our train car and said, 'Can I join your party?' We thought that might put a chill on us," Bob laughs, "but he came in and had a great time. We all were really tickled that we were able to see that side of him. He was really a great man," Chappuis concludes with obvious respect.

Chappuis was a pretty good man himself. This entire tale occurred after Chappuis had returned from World War II. He had served in the Air Force as an aerial gunner. He was shot down over Italy on his 21st mission and escaped capture after a number of harrowing adventures.

Not bad for a guy who couldn't run!

"We Were Just Fooled!"

The Michigan victory over Ohio State in 1969 was certainly the defining game in Bo Schembechler's career. But early in the 1969 season there were some bumps in the road. After five games into the 1969 season, the Wolverines were just 3-2. We opened with two straight wins over Vanderbilt and Washington, but then lost to Missouri before coming back to beat Purdue in our conference opener. Game five that season was in East Lansing against Michigan State.

The game against the Spartans would prove to be an eye opener for Bo and his staff. Duffy Daugherty was the revered coach of the Spartans. All season long, MSU had featured a Wishbone offensive attack. Against Michigan, they changed completely to an I Formation and had us on our heels all day. We were ranked 13th in the country, and MSU upset us 23-12. We were 3-2 for the year, and Schembechler never forgot that day for a couple of reasons.

"It was bad coaching that lost that game," Bo steamed. "There's no question about it! We were just fooled! And I'll never forget this until the day I die. Jim Young was our defensive coordinator, a great coach. Of course, he was frustrated because they had jumped from the Wishbone to the I Formation. We had prepared all Wishbone defenses. They were marching up and down the field. I remember walking up the sideline, and I grabbed Jim by the arm and I said, 'Jim, for God's sake, let's get 'em stopped.' He turned around and looked at me, his face turned white as a sheet, and he fainted! *Right there in front of me, he fainted!* We had to get him revived and back up to coach the rest of the game!"

It turned out that Young was OK, but that was the kind of stress that Michigan State put on the staff that afternoon. It was also, as Bo puts it, "my indoctrination to the Michigan State series."

Bo has said that when he came to Michigan, his primary focus was to bring his program to a level where it could compete with Ohio State. In his first year he installed the Ohio State offense and the Ohio State defense. He wanted his team to see it every day in practice. He wanted his team to be able to defend and block anything

Ohio State could throw at them. The Buckeyes were the power in the conference at the time, and Bo's strategy was to be able to beat them at their own game. The strategy worked beautifully, too, but he had miscalculated the impact of the Michigan State rivalry. The loss to the Spartans in 1969 really opened his eyes.

It opened them so much that Bo was virtually unbeatable against MSU during the rest of his career. After that first loss in 1969, Schembechler's Michigan teams won the next eight straight games in the series. In his 21 years at the helm of the Wolverines, Bo only lost four games to Michigan State.

"Oh, That's Too Bad"

Don Dufek played fullback for Michigan in the old single wing days in the late 1940s. He came to Michigan in 1947 as a freshman from Chicago and was a solid football player who wanted to try his luck as a Wolverine. It was a smart decision, because he turned out to be one of Michigan's best. He played on a national championship team in 1948 as a sophomore, and became a regular on two Big Ten championship teams in his junior and senior seasons. But if it weren't for a rainy day at practice at the start of his sophomore season, Don Dufek may never have played a down in the Maize and Blue.

"I didn't have a very good freshman year," Dufek remembers. "I was one of those guys who had a tough adjustment between high school and college. The maturity part of the adjustment was not one of my strong suits. It took me a little while to get tuned in to the real world of college football," Dufek laughs.

"I did finally make the team as a sophomore, but I was with the lowest of the lows in preseason practice, and things weren't looking good," says Dufek. "In those days, during the first few practices, Coach Oosterbaan tuned up the offense real well first, then we'd emphasize the defense. Well, when we started to work on the defense, all the big stars were out there, and they were going to scrimmage against the lowest of the lows. Since I was the fullback on the lowest of the lows, that meant I was in the scrimmage."

Dufek says that as the scrimmage started, the weather changed. It got windy, and the rain started. "In the single wing," Dufek recalls, "the fullback handled the ball a lot. We couldn't run a lot of the offense because of the wind and rain, so we went from the T Formation, and they'd pitch out to the left and right to the full back. I got the ball going one way and then the other. I carried it a lot, and I had a great afternoon."

Despite his great practice, Dufek says he was still thinking that he would soon be heading back home to Chicago. "I wasn't eating on the training table, and my money was running out," Dufek says with a laugh. "So that afternoon after practice, I just happened to be in the shower, and Coach Oosterbaan came in and showered next to me. He said, 'Nice going kid, you did a good job today. Keep up the good work.'"

"I said, 'Gee, thanks Coach, but I can't stay more than another day or so, because I don't have any more money to feed myself.'"

"Bennie looked at me," Dufek remembers, "and said, 'Oh, that's too bad.' And he walked out." Dufek laughs out loud as he remembers the moment.

Don Dufek thought he had just experienced his best day, and last day, as a Wolverine. It came in a practice scrimmage. "I didn't think any more about it," Dufek recalls, "until the next morning practice. Don Robinson, one of the assistant coaches, came up to me and said, 'Dufek, you start eating on the training table at noon today.'"

It was a smart decision by Oosterbaan and Robinson, no doubt. Dufek not only went on to star at Michigan as a player, but he also became a fine assistant coach for 12 years, serving under Oosterbaan and Bump Elliott. Additionally, two of Don's sons played for the Wolverines in a great family story from Michigan Stadium.

"I Was in Ninth Grade"

Throughout this collection of tales, we have covered the Michigan victory over Ohio State in 1969 a great deal. Clearly, it was a watershed event in Michigan football history. I was on the Michigan team that day. I know what an important event it was in my life. It was an important event in the lives of my teammates and coaches, too.

It surprised me, though, when I found out that a ninth-grader who was at that game said it changed the course of his life as well. That ninth-grader was Donny Dufek, the son of Don Dufek, the man who played for Michigan in the late 1940s.

"The game that epitomizes Michigan football to me was that 1969 game," Donny says. "I was in ninth grade. I was one of the kids on the sidelines who worked with the network TV spotters. I was the little guy who carried the cord for the spotters who called information up to the press box.

"I got to get an upfront look at game day, and all the pageantry and the great players, right on the field," Donny says. "That was the game that wasn't supposed to happen. Ohio State had the best team of all time. To be in ninth grade and watching Michigan football growing up, it was really special. I've never seen that Stadium like that to this day. The electricity in that place was unbelievable.

"I was at that age, like every little kid who wants to play football," Dufek remembers, "that I could visualize, potentially, that if I was good enough, and had the skill to compete in that Stadium, I wanted to be there. I mean, that was my favorite game of all time."

Donny Dufek used that game he witnessed as a ninth-grader to propel himself into the Maize and Blue winged helmet. He was indeed good enough and had the skill to compete in that Stadium. Not only did he compete, he became a team captain, and an All-America defensive back in his senior season.

He not only played football, but was also an outstanding hockey player for the Wolverines. After his career at Michigan came to a close, he moved on to the NFL with the Seattle Seahawks.

All of it was spurred on by an unforgettable afternoon he spent at Michigan Stadium as a ninth grader.

Donny Dufek follows in his dad's footsteps.

The Championship Trophy

One of the strangest tales from Michigan Stadium revolves around the Big Ten championship trophy. It was the 1993 season, and prior to the Michigan-Ohio State game, the Buckeyes had wrapped up the Big Ten title. For some reason, the Big Ten office had sent the trophy to Michigan's equipment manager, Jon Falk. Jon was told by a conference representative to make sure Ohio State got the trophy when they arrived on Friday at Michigan Stadium prior to the game.

"On Friday afternoon, before the game," Jon recalls, "I went to their locker room after Ohio State had arrived for their practice and looked for their coaches. When I found them, I told them that the Big Ten had sent the trophy to me to deliver to them. I gave it to them, and they put it out in the visiting locker room at the Stadium."

Jon says that is when the game the next day started to go Michigan's way. "As the Ohio State players walked out of the locker room to practice, they all stood and stared at that trophy. They stopped and touched it. As they walked down the tunnel to practice, they were all talking about the trophy. They said things like, 'This is our trophy. We won this trophy.' Even the coaches would grab it and hold it up and show it to the players," Jon remembers.

The reaction to the trophy by Ohio State struck Jon as a bit odd. "I remember thinking to myself," Jon says, "this is like feeding grain to croppies. These guys are coming in here and they think they own this place. It was unbelievable! I thought to myself, Bo [Schembechler] or Mo [Gary Moeller] would never let this happen. If either of them had seen that trophy, they would have gotten ahold of me and told me to take that trophy in the back room and not to let anybody see it. They would have said, 'We haven't won anything until we beat Ohio State.'

"Not Ohio State," Jon goes on. "They had to see it. They had to touch it."

Gary Moeller was the head coach for the Wolverines at the time. Jon says that after Ohio State finished practice, he locked up

A trophy like this was Ohio State's undoing according to Jon Falk.

at the Stadium and rushed over to the football office to see Moeller. "I told Mo," Jon says with a smile, "this game is over. We've won this game. Then I told him the story about the trophy and the Ohio State reaction."

People around Michigan football will tell you that Jon Falk is quite a character. In this instance, not only was he a character, he was a prophet. Ohio State entered the game ranked fifth in the country, but they left with a big goose egg. Moeller took his Wolverines into Michigan Stadium that Saturday and used the story Jon told him as part of a motivational message to his team. Michigan demolished Ohio State 28-0.

Walter Weber

There is no way that you can write about Michigan Stadium or Michigan football without including the name of Walter Weber. When I enrolled at Michigan in 1968, "Wally" Weber was still around and still a regular visitor around the football offices. He was in demand as a speaker and a favorite at pep rallies. Who can forget Wally Weber rolling his pant legs up to his knees as the student body roared before he spoke so eloquently about his beloved Michigan?

During the late 1960s, Wally was an elder statesman and quite a character. I am told he enjoyed the occasional cocktail, and he was a master storyteller. He loved nothing more than to wrap himself around a hot toddy and regale his guests with tales about the legends who were his contemporaries.

Weber was the starting fullback on the last team Fielding Yost coached at Michigan. Then, from 1931 to 1958, Wally was on the Michigan football coaching staff. He was coaching before the winged helmet was designed by Crisler, and he was there long after it became the trademark of Michigan football. There aren't many left who remember Wally Weber, but Hercules Renda, a fine halfback for Michigan in the late 1930s, is one of them. "Wally Weber was the ideal freshman coach," Renda states without hesitation.

"Wally would never call you by your first name," Renda says. "He would call you by the place you were from, and the state you were from. Can you imagine? Think of the memory that man had.

"He would always use those big words," Renda laughs. "That was Wally. You were perfectly at ease with him at any time."

Renda remembers that Weber loved coaching so much he even found a way to coach the student body who weren't on the football team. "There was a time," Renda says, "when the freshman students who were physical education majors had a football team. Wally Weber would coach those students in the morning, and in the afternoon he would go down to Ferry Field and coach his freshman football team. The last day of practice would then be a game between those two teams. As a matter of fact," Renda recalls, "I think the last game on the old Ferry Field was a game between

Wally Weber: "How are you, my taxpayin' friends?"

the freshman physical education majors and the freshman football squad, and Wally coached both teams. "

Renda says his team beat the physical education team in that game 7-0.

"He could inspire you," Renda says about Weber.

Not only could Wally inspire you, he could also keep you in stitches of laughter. His pattern of speech was unique. His vocabulary was immense. If you wanted a good laugh, all you needed to do was hang around Wally for a while, and the laughs would soon follow.

In December 1969, some of Wally's friends staged a testimonial dinner for him. One of those friends was Don Robinson, a former player and fellow coach with Wally at Michigan. Robinson wisely kept the program from that night, and he was kind enough to send me a copy. The program included some of the "Weberisms" that made Wally famous. What follows is a sample of Wally Weber's special brand of eloquence:

"Michigan—Shrine of Minerva, Athens of the West, Fount of Learning."

"He was hit so hard, he took a short course in astronomy, 'Stars over Ann Arbor.'"

"Dean of action, Dean of the latrine, and test pilot for Seagram's."

"It is indeed a pleasure to regale you in doubtful Ciceronian rhetoric."

"Do you follow me, or am I like the balcony—over your head?"

"Their punter is like their alumni—always kicking."

"Some sportsmen consider bending over to tie their shoes an athletic event."

"Longest pass in the world—from pole to pole—Mazakowski to Jankowski."

"Colder than a mother-in-law's osculation."

"How are you, my taxpayin' friends?"

"He's like the farmer, out standing in his field."

He may be one of the less remembered of Michigan Stadium, but Wally Weber belongs in the same category as Yost and Crisler and the rest of the legends. Michigan Stadium has seen many a great one, but when you are asked, don't forget to include Wally Weber in the list of benevolent ghosts that still live in the aura that surrounds Michigan Stadium.

We Were Near Tears

During the Schembechler years at Michigan, it became clear to everyone that being late was not a good thing. Whether it was a meeting or practice, being late was not an option. Invariably, though, there came a time when someone would test the waters of promptness. It didn't matter whether the tardiness had a legitimate reason or not; arriving late to anything Bo was involved with meant swift punishment. Instead of being on Eastern Standard Time, we operated on BST—Bo Schembechler Time.

This tale involves a couple of freshmen who were well aware of the on-time requirements, but who got caught in circumstances beyond their control.

Linebacker Ron Simpkins and receiver Ralph Clayton were having lunch at the dorm in their first year on the Friday before the Ohio State game in Columbus. Neither of them was wearing a watch. Clayton had forgotten something in his room, so they both went to the room to retrieve the item. When they returned to the front of the dorm, all the other players were gone, so they couldn't hitch a ride. Neither Simpkins nor Clayton had a car. They started the walk down State Street to the football building. The buses were waiting there to take the team to the airport for the quick flight to Columbus.

Simpkins remembers not having a sense of being late until they got near the football building. "At about Hoover and State, we looked up and saw these buses pulling out of the lot down by the practice field about a two blocks away," Simpkins says. "We thought it must be a bus of fans. Then about three more buses pulled away following the first one, and we knew that many fans weren't leaving this early to the game, so we started running. We had our bags with us, and sport coats on. The next thing you know, we're standing in the parking lot, and there is no team and no buses, just a couple of alumni."

"Ralph and I were on the verge of tears," Simpkins laughs. "One of the alumni took pity on us and agreed to give us a ride to the airport. So we finally got to the gate, the team buses pulled through and right on to the tarmac, but the guard wouldn't let us through. We showed him our Michigan travel blazers and pleaded with him that we were on the team and that we had to get to the plane. We were in tears again, and he finally let us through."

Simpkins says at this point they thought they had avoided disaster. "We figured that we were going to make it and nobody was going to know," Simpkins recalls, "but the guy driving us pulled right up in front of the first bus and dropped us off. We couldn't drop in behind the rest of the team boarding, and who was standing at the top of the stairs? *Bo!* He gave us a scowl. It was the worst scowl we'd ever seen in our lives.

"Well, we got on the plane," Simpkins laughs, "and as we were walking down the aisle, Bo poked both of us in the chest with his finger and said, 'I want to see you guys when we get to Ohio State.'"

Simpkins says both he and Clayton were sweating bullets on the plane ride to Columbus. "I was thinking where I might be able to transfer," Simpkins says with a chuckle. "And the scariest thing was that Bo never said a word to us the entire flight down there or on the bus to the hotel.

"When we finally arrived at the hotel, he summoned us," Simpkins says. "All I remember about that meeting was verbal abuse. All we could do was say we were sorry. After a few minutes, Bo said, 'You're not sorry *yet*. You'll be sorry when you get back, and we better win this game, too!'"

Simpkins says they played the game, and Michigan did win. The victory gave them the Big Ten championship and a trip to the Rose Bowl. But Simpkins and Clayton were still waiting for the other shoe to drop.

It dropped not long after they returned to Ann Arbor. "Every morning at six, Clayton and I had to go down to the practice field and run a mile," Simpkins remembers painfully. "It had to be for two or two and a half weeks, until we left for the Rose Bowl, we had to run at six every day. We ran during final exams and everything!" Simpkins exclaims.

According to Ron, there was no reprieve, either. "I remember one morning when it was snowing like you couldn't believe. There must have been six feet of snow outside," Ron exaggerates for emphasis. "And the assistant coaches had to rotate with us. Each day a different coach would meet us and watch us run. So on this snowy morning, Ralph and I thought we'd get out of it. They wouldn't make us run in a snowstorm!

"Tom Reed, a defensive assistant, was there to meet us this particular day. We told him, 'Well, we can't run today, it's too snowy.'"

"Reed said, 'If I've got to get up at six in the morning with you guys, then you guys are going to run!' And we had to go out there and run in the snow," Simpkins remembers. "So there we are at six in the morning running around. We were the only two people outside!"

The whole incident may sound a little severe, but it sure got the attention of the offenders. Simpkins and Clayton had their morning runs cancelled once they arrived in California for the Rose Bowl preparations, but Simpkins says he sure learned his lesson. "I never missed another bus. I was never late for anything again! I was always early from that point on," Simpkins laughs. "And I stopped hanging around with Ralph, too."

The Difference Between Then and Now

It's no secret that there is a huge difference between collegiate football in the 1940s and 1950s and what we see today. The players are bigger, stronger, and faster. There is a great deal more emphasis on the games and players because of the economics involved. It's

Photo courtesy of Bentley Historical Library, University of Michigan

Don Dufek (far right) kneels with the 1954 coaching staff.

always nice to go back to a more innocent time and hear the tales of what it used to be like before the pressure cooker got turned up.

One of these stories comes from Don Dufek, who played in the late 1940s and coached at Michigan through the 1950s and 1960s. Dufek remembers a story told by a teammate of his that illustrates how times have changed for players.

In the old days, on Friday nights before games, the Michigan team would stay at the U of M golf course clubhouse. The upper floor of the clubhouse was a barracks of sorts, with upper and lower bunk beds. After early-evening meetings on the main floor, players would start to move upstairs to bed. Nowadays, the team stays at the Campus Inn on Friday nights before home games, and each player has his own double bed.

Dufek says that on one occasion, a sophomore named Pete Kinyon from Ann Arbor went off to bed at the golf course a little earlier than the rest of the guys. "Kinyon was assigned to the same bunk as Dick McWilliams, a senior guard," Dufek recalls. "So when McWilliams gets upstairs to go to bed, he sees Kinyon sleeping in the lower bunk! McWilliams wakes him up and says, 'Kinyon, what do you think you're doing? You're just a lousy sophomore. You don't get the lower bunk; get upstairs!' Well, Kinyon apologizes and moves to the upper bunk," Dufek laughs.

From that point, everything goes normally for the rest of the night. But, Dufek recalls, at a very early hour on Saturday, McWilliams hears rustling coming from the bunk above him. "McWilliams wakes up and it's like five in the morning!" Dufek says. "Here is Kinyon getting out of bed and getting dressed. McWilliams asks him, 'What in the hell are you doing?'

"Kinyon says in a hushed voice so he wouldn't wake anybody, 'I've got to go do my newspaper route,'" Dufek recalls with a laugh. "'What the hell do you mean,' McWilliams says. 'You've got a big game today. You play football for the University of Michigan. You're not going to do any newspaper route on a day like this.'"

Dufek says Kinyon was beside himself, and he told McWilliams, "I've been doing this paper route since I was in junior high school, and I've got to get these papers delivered."

Dufek says he doesn't remember whether Kinyon got the papers delivered, but he never forgot the story. As Dufek told me, "It's just a great story that illustrates the difference between then and now."

"I'm Sorry Coach, I'll Be Right Back"

Michigan Stadium on a game day can elicit a number of emotional responses. Back in the mid-1980s, the experience of an opponent of Michigan was not so pleasant. It had nothing to do with the game he was about to play. It had more to do with the impressive sight of that stadium filling up with people and the anticipation of what lay ahead.

A current Michigan assistant coach, Fred Jackson, was coaching at Wisconsin when this particular event happened, and he says he'll never forget it. "We come in to play Michigan, and I'm coaching the quarterbacks and receivers," Jackson recalls. "We had come out on the field to warm up. We'd thrown the ball around, gotten warmed up, and then came out again with the full team. Well, not long after we get out there, my quarterback starts to leave and head back up the tunnel. I see this and ask him where he's going, and he says, 'I'm sorry Coach. I'll be right back. I just wet my pants.'"

Jackson says he was just about speechless. "I said, 'What!'" Fred recalls, "and the kid looked at me and said, 'Coach, I've never seen this many people together in my life. They're yelling and screaming either for you or against you, and I just couldn't hold it.' That was my first experience," Jackson says with chuckle, "where I saw how Michigan Stadium affected someone else.

"I thought we had a great chance to win that day," Jackson said about that game with the Wolverines, "but when that happened, I knew we were in trouble.

"That was my first major experience in the Stadium," laughs Fred. "And actually, the kid went on to play a pretty good game."

Despite his good game, the quarterback, Jackson, and the Badgers lost to Michigan. But Jackson will never forget the events before the game, and the effect the Stadium had on his player. I don't imagine the quarterback will ever forget either.

"I Completely Stopped"

It's hard to imagine the different kinds of emotions that Michigan Stadium can generate in young men taking the field to play a game. It is a bit different when you are wearing the Maize and Blue and Michigan Stadium is your home field. Everyone experiences a

Stanley Edwards realized his dream playing for Michigan.

different emotion, unique to themselves. The one constant in the mix of emotion is that no player who ever took that field on a home game Saturday will ever forget it.

Stanley Edwards was a top-flight running back out of the Detroit Public School League. He is one of those who experienced the first run out of the tunnel, and the moment has never left him. "I had sat in the stands two years earlier," remembers Edwards, "when I was being recruited. But it was so different when we played our first home game my freshman year.

"It was after pregame warmups," Stan says, "so we had already been out there. We started down the tunnel, and we knew the Stadium was full. Way back at the top of the tunnel, you can hear the guy on the public address system introducing the starting lineups. When you look down the tunnel, the opening seems so small, and you start heading down to the field like a herd of cattle."

At that point Stan says he started to think back to his days growing up. "I thought to myself, 'Oh my God, I've been working for this all of my life, and here it is!'

"I was at the back of the line," Stan recalls, "because I was a freshman. So when we came out of the tunnel into the sunlight to touch the banner, I took about two steps and completely stopped. I could not hear anything. I just stopped and stared into the stands. Somebody finally grabbed me and yelled, 'C'mon, c'mon, lets go!' And I came out of my trance, jumped up to touch the banner, and jumped on the pile of players in front of the bench.

"After we broke the huddle in front of the bench," Edwards remembers, "I went back to staring. For about the first two series, I just stood there on the bench and stared at the people in the Stadium. I thought it was absolutely amazing. At a PSL game you may get maybe 300 to 500 people, and here I was with over 100,000 people around me. I literally froze.

"It was a good thing I wasn't playing, because I wouldn't have been able to play," laughs Edwards.

Stan Edwards got over his stage fright at Michigan Stadium quickly enough. He became a regular starter not long after that first run down the tunnel, and was a standout on two Big Ten championship teams. He also scored the game-clincher at the Rose Bowl in 1981, which just happened to be Schembechler's first win in the New Year's Day classic.

That Set the Table

Another great story about the tunnel at Michigan Stadium and waiting to explode onto the field comes from my teammate and All-America guard Reggie McKenzie. To understand the story, though, you've got to go back to our freshman year, 1968.

Unable to play as freshmen, by rule, Reggie and I and the freshman team, all gathered together at Crisler Arena for the Ohio State-Michigan game in Columbus. A big screen had been set up to show the game on closed circuit for the student body, and we were all there anticipating a win. As many of you know, it was a crushing loss, 50-14. Adding insult to injury, Woody Hayes had gone for a two-point conversion at the end of that game with a big lead to rub it in, and it rubbed all of us the wrong way. "That set the table for me," Reggie says.

As sophomores in 1969, we had the Ohio State game in the backs of our minds, but with a new coach in Bo Schembechler and learning a new system, we had plenty to think about without obsessing on Ohio State. We were learning about the Michigan tradition, but it hadn't hit home yet. It was still just a concept. We had nothing concrete to stand on. We were just surviving our sophomore year. We were unaware of the legacy that was about to be passed down to us.

Reggie McKenzie remembers when it became more than just a concept to him. It happened in the tunnel prior to the Ohio State game in 1969. "We were just 19- and 20-year-old young men," Reggie says. "We didn't understand what Michigan football was all about. It really hit home for me in that tunnel at Michigan Stadium in 1969 before Ohio State. I get emotional even now talking about it," Reggie says with enthusiasm.

"What we didn't realize as sophomores that day was what those juniors, who were now seniors, had said to Ron Johnson and Tom Goss after the Ohio State game the previous year. They had all cried in the locker room at Ohio State. They had told the seniors who wouldn't be coming back not to worry. 'We'll pay them back!'"

Ron Johnson verified that story about Columbus. "Oh yeah, we were all crying. We couldn't believe what had happened," Johnson says. "The game in 1968 was so much closer than the score. Then to have Woody do what he did. For that to be our last game was terrible. And the juniors all came over and told me, 'Don't worry, we're going to kick their ass next year. They will pay for this!'"

Clearly, the juniors were on a mission, and in their senior year, they carried it out. Reggie McKenzie, as a sophomore, didn't understand the resolve his upper-class teammates had until that Saturday in 1969. "I was standing at the top of the tunnel," Reggie recalls, "and I saw our captain, Jim Mandich, with tears coming down his face. I looked out the tunnel at Ohio State, and they looked at us, and I swear, they knew they had an ass-whupping coming.

"What I finally realized about the Michigan tradition in that moment," Reggie continues, "is that Mandich and those seniors had to depend on the juniors and sophomores to help them keep their promise to Ron Johnson and the other seniors that they had made the year before. At that particular point in time, I grew up. It became my promise, too. I became part of the tradition.

"Mandich showed me," Reggie says, "where I had to get emotionally, to play the game. That was the greatest game I've ever participated in. I only played one play, and I got my man.

"A lot of great things have happened to me in my lifetime," McKenzie goes on. "I mean, God has been very good to me, but the greatest thing that has ever happened to me is Michigan. I'll never forget, as long as I live, that moment in the tunnel. It changed my life."

Reggie McKenzie learned about tradition against Ohio State in 1969.

As you well know, Michigan went on to win the game 24-12 in a huge upset. Jim Mandich and the other seniors fulfilled their promise to Ron Johnson. "I remember I was in Cleveland," Johnson recalls, "playing for the New York Giants, getting ready to play the Browns. I can't tell you how proud I was of those guys as I watched the game. I just laughed and laughed and laughed.

"Every one of them told me in 1968, 'Don't worry about it, we'll take care of it,'" Johnson says with a smile. "And they did!"

For Ron Johnson, it was sweet revenge even though he didn't participate in the game. For Reggie McKenzie, it was more than just a win. It was about his passage from football player to Michigan football player. There is a difference. It took a senior captain in tears to drive the message home. It was received loud and clear. And the Michigan tradition was dutifully carried on.

The Compassionate Side

Football is a tough, physical game. Invariably, injuries occur to players. No amount of conditioning or training can keep you safe from injury. If it happens, it happens, and you have to deal with it and move on. This next tale from Michigan Stadium centers around an injury and a great comeback from that injury.

Michigan had completed an 8-3 season in 1979 and headed to the Gator Bowl in Jacksonville, Florida to take on North Carolina. John Wangler had earned the starting quarterback job late in the season, and he got the start against the Tar Heels. In the early going, it was a big play kind of game, and Wangler was having a great start. Then the injury factor hit Wangler. He was smashed and suffered a nasty knee injury. Surgery would be required. Wangler was lost for the rest of the game. Michigan fell to the Lawrence Taylor-led Tar Heels 17-15.

Wangler's knee injury was a major topic of discussion in the offseason. Most felt that he would not be ready. Still others felt it may have been a career-ending injury. Wangler was not having any of the talk. He worked extremely hard and rehabilitated the knee so that when practice started the next fall, he was ready to go. Still, there were doubters, and one of them was head coach Bo Schembechler.

"I had all the medical clearances," Wangler says, "but Bo was reluctant to put me in because of the knee. It was really nice to see that he was so concerned. You know, everybody thinks college football, at that level, is such a meat market. But Bo was genuinely concerned. He kept asking me, 'Are you sure?'"

"A lot of people never saw the compassionate side of Bo," Wangler continued. "He felt that way about everybody. I kept telling him that I was OK, any time he would ask."

After an opening game win against Northwestern that saw Rich Hewlett get the start at quarterback, the Wolverines traveled to Notre Dame. Trailing at the half against the Irish, Bo finally made the move to Wangler. "I'll never forget," Wangler remembers. "Bo called all the offensive linemen together and said, 'I don't want anybody from Notre Dame laying a hand on Wangler.' That was special to me," John finishes.

Wangler's injury also forced a little change in the offense. The knee did inhibit Wangler's mobility somewhat, so the option running game had to be shelved. It wasn't shelved completely, but Bo didn't go to it as often as he had when Hewlett was at quarterback. It also became a point of contention between Wangler and Schembechler.

Wangler led Michigan to the Big Ten title in 1980, and his knee held up just fine. A trip to the Rose Bowl followed. Michigan went on to win that game against Washington for the first Bowl victory in Bo's Michigan career. In that Rose Bowl game, though, the option play, Wangler's knee, and Bo's reluctance to call Wang's number on a running play resurfaced.

"I hadn't scored all year," Wangler laughs, "so in the Rose Bowl, Bo wanted to get me a touchdown. It was second down and goal to go on the Washington three-yard line, and Bo called an option. I got down to about the half-yard line, but didn't make it in. I told Bo to call it again. He said, 'Forget you!' And we gave it to Stan Edwards up the middle and he scored," Wangler laughs. "He gave me my one shot, but he didn't want to screw around anymore. Bo said, 'That's it!'"

Wangler says he told Bo if he did score he was going to spike the ball anyway, which was a no-no. They both got a big laugh over that one. And it was all so much sweeter since Wangler and Bo had a 23-6 Rose Bowl win in the bag.

It was quite a year for Wangler and Michigan in 1980. "Wangs" had struggled back from the knee surgery, regained his starting position after being unsure he would ever play again, and led Michigan to a Rose Bowl win. It was more than he could have hoped for. And all of the struggles and trials of his career hit home in his last game at Michigan Stadium.

Even before his near-score in the Rose Bowl, Wangler says the memory of his final game in The Big House is something that he'll never forget. "As a senior going out, it's so emotional," Wangler remembers. "It's the last time you run out of the tunnel. It's the last time you jump up and touch the banner. We were playing Purdue. If they had beaten us, they would have gone to the Rose Bowl. Mark Herrman was their quarterback. If he had a good game, he might

John Wangler (No. 5): Bad knee and all,
he became one of Michigan's finest quarterbacks.

have won the Heisman. But, what I remember about that day was warming up before the game. I was in tears warming up. There was so much emotion. I was crying, and they put a TV camera right in my face.

"We all were crying," Wangler says emotionally, "all of the seniors were crying. It was such an emotional day, and then we shut Purdue out. It was really special!"

They Were Playing the Alma Mater

Emotional experiences at Michigan Stadium make a pattern that repeats itself over the years. From the very beginning of Michigan football to the modern player of today, emotions have overwhelmed young men wearing the Maize and Blue.

It was a particularly emotional time for players and fans alike in the mid-1940s at the conclusion of World War II. Many of the players were veterans of the great conflict. To be back home on U.S. soil and back to a normal existence was, in many cases, too much for a young man to handle without getting emotional.

Bob Chappuis, a Wolverine All-America halfback and war hero, remembers such a moment. "We were playing Army in 1946," Chappuis recalls. "They had [Doc] Blanchard and [Glenn] Davis. And they beat us 20-13 at Michigan Stadium. But I'll never forget coming out at halftime. The band was still on the field. They were playing the alma mater. I stood there next to Bruce Hilkene, and I had tears running down my cheeks.

"I though to myself, 'Gee whiz, I can't do this,'" Chappuis recalls with some embarrassment. "But then I looked at Bruce, and there were tears running down his cheeks, too.

"I'm an emotional guy anyway," Chappuis continues. "Someone once said to me that I would choke up watching jackpot bowling, but believe me, I never will forget that moment. Looking up and seeing all those people, I thought, 'My gosh, isn't this something!'

You know, you just can't believe it. You just can't believe the grip that Stadium has on you."

We get the idea, thanks to you, Bob.

"Well, We Got You, Fat Man!"

Dave Fisher was a fullback for Michigan in the mid-1960s. He wasn't your prototype fullback, either. He stood only about five foot 10 and weighed in the neighborhood of 210 pounds. He was your basic fireplug kind of guy. He had a very low center of gravity and was as tough as they come.

Dave also had a unique personality. He'd say just about anything to anybody and think about the consequences later. He was a great guy to have as a teammate. If you wanted to go to war with someone, you'd pick Fisher in the first round to be in the foxhole next to you.

Fisher grew up in Dayton, Ohio, but managed to find his way to Ann Arbor and play for the Maize and Blue, despite being recruited heavily to go to Ohio State by Woody Hayes. "Actually, I spent more time in Columbus than I had anyplace else in the world before I came to Ann Arbor," remembers Fisher. "Being an Ohio kid, I wanted to beat Ohio State and Woody as bad as anything. So we're in Columbus, moving down the field, and I get knocked out of bounds right at Woody's feet. I look up at him and say, 'Well, we got you, fat man.'

"I honestly don't know why I said it," Fisher says today, "but that's what I said, and he spit at me! My teammate, Frank Nunley, couldn't believe I did it either, and we've had yuks about that forever."

Fisher escaped Ohio State that day, but you can see the kind of personality David brought with him to a game. In another instance during Fisher's career, he spoke to another coach. Only this time, the laugh was on Fisher.

It was a game against Illinois at Michigan Stadium. At the time, Bump Elliott was the Michigan coach, and his brother Pete

Dave Fisher (No. 33) could run hard, as well as talk.

was coaching the Illini. "Back in those days," Fisher recalls, "the tunnel at Michigan Stadium had a dirt floor. It was really dusty. Well, coming down the tunnel before the game, I was sweaty, it was dusty, and my eyes were burning. I couldn't see very well anyway, and the conditions made it worse. We were standing in the tunnel, waiting to roar out on the field, when I looked over and saw Bump standing next to me. He appeared a little nervous through the dust and sweat in my eyes, so I said, 'Don't worry Coach, we're going to kick their ass for you today.' He turned, looked back at me, smiled and said, 'I'm *not* your Coach!'

"*It was Pete!*" Fisher laughed. "They looked so much alike anyway that with the dirt and sweat hurting my eyes I really couldn't tell."

According to Fisher, Pete got his measure of revenge that afternoon. It was during that game that Dick Vidmer threw the untimely interception to the Illini's Bruce Sullivan, who returned it 99 yards for a touchdown, still a record against Michigan, in a 28-21 Illinois victory. Fisher remembers the play well. "I chased that SOB the entire 99 yards, too."

The Potato Chip Truck

I thought long and hard about including this story, because it concerns me and my weight. You may be wondering what this has to do with Michigan Stadium, but I'll let you decide. It's just one of those humorous stories about getting ready to play college football at Michigan with Bo Schembechler as the supreme ruler.

We must first return to the days of yesteryear when Bo first arrived in Ann Arbor. It was just after the first of the year, in 1969. Bo had just been named the head coach, and a bunch of us players went down to the football building to see the press conference. After it was all over, we lined up in a kind of reception line to meet him. As I got to Bo and introduced myself for the first time, he shook my hand, then grabbed a pinch of flesh above my belt and said, "You could stand to lose some weight."

That was the beginning of a constant struggle between the supreme ruler and yours truly about my weight. Bo was a real stickler about our weight. We all had to report at the designated weight that Bo and the staff determined. In that first year, he told us that he didn't want anyone over 250 pounds. For 99 percent of the team the 250-pound number was no problem but, for Dan Dierdorf and me, the fear was palpable.

You've got to understand, Dan was a big man. He was thick. Large boned and wide, Dierdorf at 250 pounds looked emaciated. It was different for me. I was just chunky. Nonetheless, we both reported at our designated weight. I can guarantee you that we didn't finish at that same weight.

As I got into my junior and senior years, the weight became more and more difficult to keep under control. It was a constant issue between Bo and me. It never failed that after spring football drills were completed, and we all headed home for the summer, Bo would search me out and make it clear, in no uncertain terms, that he wanted me back in the fall, *in shape*!

During our summer breaks, Bo and the staff would keep track of us. They wanted to be sure we had good safe jobs and were working out so we'd return to Ann Arbor in top physical condition

Not bad for a potato chip truck driver, eh?

for the upcoming season. These checkups were handled for Bo by the position coaches. Jerry Hanlon was the offensive line coach, so he had to keep tabs on me. Little did I know that Jerry's job was hanging in the balance, according to what Bo told him, if I came back heavy and out of shape. So Hanlon was on me pretty hard.

It just so happened that one summer, my brother Art had obtained the distribution rights in Lansing, Michigan, to Charles Chips. If you don't know about Charles Chips, let me fill you in. They are, without a doubt, some of the best potato chips ever produced by man. They also had a line of pretzels and other goodies.

These chips and pretzels came in cans, and they were delivered door to door. When I got home that summer, Art asked me if I'd like to work for him as a kind of general manager for Charles Chips in Lansing for the summer. The job meant I would map delivery routes, market the product to new customers, and deliver the chips. I thought it was a great deal. I was driving around town in a big step-van with Charles Chips emblazoned on the side panels, and inside the van was a stockpile of outstanding product.

Well, when Jerry Hanlon called one day and asked what I had landed for my summer job, and I told him, the phone went dead silent. After a moment of this silence, Hanlon used some interesting language in explaining to me that this had better not cause a problem with my weight. As I recall, the phrase "fox in a hen house" was used repeatedly. I assured Coach Hanlon it was not a problem, and he shouldn't worry. He wasn't convinced. Neither was I.

I went about my job, and I must confess, I had occasion to sample the product. Unbeknownst to me, Hanlon had covered for me with Bo as long as he could. Jerry told me once that when Bo asked him how I was doing he would dance around the job issue and reassure Bo that I was going to report in shape.

According to Jerry, one day Bo asked him point blank, "So what's Brandstatter's job this summer?" Jerry had no room to dance, so he told him I was driving a potato chip truck. Hanlon tells me the concussion from the explosion could be felt in Toledo.

That night, Jerry called me at home and told me with resignation that Bo was not real happy, and if I didn't come back at my designated weight, and in shape, both of us could kiss our careers good-bye.

Of course I knew Bo was never going to blame Jerry for my conditioning, but I owed it to Hanlon to keep the heat off. I also knew that my life would be a lot easier if I buckled down and put the chips aside. So, about two and a half weeks before we were to report, I went up north to my parents' home on Lake Huron. It was my two-week retreat for conditioning.

Nobody knew where I was. I worked out three times a day. I ran sprints in the sand wearing combat boots in the morning. I exercised with push-ups and jumping jacks and sit-ups at mid-day.

In the late afternoon, I returned to running sprints and jogging distance. I ate lettuce, and one ground beef patty, and more lettuce as a daily diet. I don't recommend this diet for anyone, but I was under the gun.

When I returned to Ann Arbor a couple of days prior to our official report date, I stopped by the offices to see Bo and Jerry. When Hanlon looked at me, he breathed an audible sigh of relief. I had lost about 18 pounds and looked solid. When I saw Bo, he pinched me above the belt like he did that first time I met him and said, "I am somewhat impressed."

For the official weigh-in, I was a couple of pounds over, and I had to get up at 6 a.m. during double sessions and run penalty miles, but I had avoided a major meltdown.

As the season went along, my weight fluctuated, and we had to get weighed in at regular intervals. The weigh-ins were traumatic. But an offensive guard named Tom Coyle came to my rescue. Actually, Tommy had a weight issue himself. We were both in the same predicament, and he had a plan to fix it.

Tom had come to Michigan from the South Side of Chicago. He was from a huge Irish family, and to know Tommy Coyle was to love him. He was tough as nails as a player. He had the personality of a charming con man, and you couldn't help but like him. Coyle and Jim Betts were the only two players I knew who could talk their way out of a jam with Bo and have Bo smiling about it afterward.

Tommy decided that this weigh-in regimen was way too stressful, and he was going to do something about it. So in a bit of ingenuity that would have impressed Einstein, Coyle would get small pieces of adhesive tape from the training room. He would rub them around in his hands so they became little adhesive tape balls. He would then place them under the pads on the scale. They were out of sight to anyone standing up next to the scale. The effect of these little adhesive tape balls was amazing. Coyle and I would always be first in line for the weigh-in. We would get on the scales and depress the balls of tape but we were always five to six pounds lighter, thanks to the tape. The coach checking us would dutifully write our weight down on the log and we'd move on. The guys who followed us on the scale were their proper weight, because Tommy and I had depressed the tape enough that it didn't affect the weight of those who came after us. After everybody had weighed in, and the coast was clear by the scales, we'd go back and remove the small tape balls with a ball-point pen or knife, and life was good.

I believe Coyle, Dierdorf, and I benefited most from the adhesive tape. As I told you at the top of this story, I'm not sure this qualifies as a tale from Michigan Stadium, but I do know that we never stop telling the story when we get together at reunions. You decide. Potato chip trucks and adhesive tape are not what you might expect when talking about football, but they all had a major connection for me.

Tommy Coyle (No. 60) was great with adhesive tape.

You Could Sit Anywhere You Wanted

Don Robinson wasn't 10 years old when he first saw Michigan Stadium. It just so happened that the first time he saw it also happened to be during the Stadium's first few years of existence. "My father took me into the Michigan locker room at the Stadium in 1929," Robinson remembers. "I remember seeing a preseason scrimmage in the Stadium and then walking up the tunnel with Harry Newman, Michigan's quarterback."

For Don Robinson, Michigan Stadium has been a major part of his life. After his experience as a seven-year-old, he went on to enroll at Michigan as a student in 1939 and donned the Maize and Blue as a player. After a hiatus from Michigan so he could serve his country in World War II, Robinson returned to Ann Arbor and won his last letter in 1946. He then stayed on at Michigan as an assistant coach to Fritz Crisler and Bennie Oosterbaan for nine years.

Don Robinson's history with Michigan Stadium is unique. He remembers that in the beginning, the Stadium was not filled on a regular basis. "When I played, heck, even when Harmon played, we only had maybe 35,000 or 40,000 people to every game," Robinson says. "The only time we filled it was for the Ohio State game. Capacity was only 72,000 to begin with, and then they put some temporary seats up to get it over 80,000."

Robinson laughed as he thought about tickets for the games. "The tickets, when I was a kid, were just five dollars. I remember we used to sell them for five dollars. You know, in the early days they put fences up starting at the first row in the stands at the goal-lines. The fences would go all the way up to the top of the Stadium. These fences were in both end zones. People could sit in the fenced-in area in the end zones for two dollars. It was five dollars if they wanted to sit in the stands between the two goal-lines.

"For the two-dollar seats," Robinson continued, "you could get in at either end zone in that fenced-in area and sit anywhere you wanted to."

The growth of Michigan Stadium since those early days is astounding. In 1949 when permanent steel bleachers were erected

Don Robinson performs back in his playing days.

to replace the wooden structure at the top of the Stadium, Michigan averaged an incredible 93,894 in attendance for their six home games.

In 1956, capacity was raised to 100,001 at Michigan Stadium, and the first crowd of over 100,000 to see a Michigan game occurred on October 6 of that year, when Michigan lost to Michigan State 9-0.

On November 8, 1975, Michigan Stadium hosted 102,415 fans as the Wolverines blanked Purdue 28-0. It is a significant date, because there has never been a crowd under 100,000 at Michigan Stadium for a football game since.

The current capacity at Michigan Stadium, entering the 2002 football season, is 107,501. Michigan Stadium currently holds the NCAA single-game attendance record, thanks to a crowd of 111,575 fans that witnessed a 24-17 Wolverine victory over Ohio State in 1999. In that same season, Michigan Stadium hosted an average of 111,008 fans per game for yet another NCAA record.

Of all those seats available, we'd like to add, not one of them can be bought for two dollars anymore, not even in the end zone.

The Pride of Harbor Beach

We've written a lot about Coach Schembechler and his occasional colorful language when he had a point to make, but he wasn't the only one who could twirl an adjective while coaching at Michigan. It was a bit of a surprise while talking with Bob Chappuis to find out that even coach Fritz Crisler could stop you in your tracks with the spoken word.

Fritz had a reputation as a very stern man. He was not one to rant and rave. He was always very measured in his remarks. When he did want to make a point, he had a favorite term. Bob Chappuis says a teammate of his in the early 1940s, Jim Brieske, made himself a target for Coach Crisler.

Jim Brieske was the pride of Harbor Beach.

"In the opening game of 1942, we were all sophomores, and we had beaten Great Lakes 9-0," Chappuis began. "I threw a touchdown pass in the game to Paul White. Brieske had missed the extra point but had made a field goal. Now Brieske, you understand, was from a small town called Harbor Beach in northern Michigan. Brieske had never gotten into a game at Michigan before, and he didn't get into too many after that either, except to kick field goals," Chappuis laughed.

"Anyway," Chappuis continued, "Brieske came into the locker room the next week after the game with a newspaper. It was the *Harbor Beach Chronicle* or something like that. He showed us the headline, and it read, 'Jim Brieske, the Pride of Harbor Beach.' I mean, it was a big headline," Chappuis recalled. "So he showed it to all of us, and then he went into the coaches' locker room and showed it to them. And that was a bad mistake!

"We got out to practice that day," Chappuis went on, "and Crisler put Brieske on defense. Well, he was on his back all day. We were just knocking him down on every play. He was a linebacker, and without being too nasty, he wasn't a very good one. I mean, time after time, he was on his back, and finally, Crisler went over to him while he's lying there and said, 'Brieske, you're not the pride of Harbor Beach, you're a jackass.'" Chappuis laughed out loud as he related the story.

"You know, that was the only bad thing Fritz would ever say," Chappuis concluded. "I mean he never swore or anything. But, if you were real bad, he'd call you a double jackass!"

"It Gives Me Goose Bumps!"

In recent history at Michigan Stadium there have been wonderful moments and difficult moments. But there is no greater moment for Lloyd Carr than the finish of the 1997 season when his Wolverines completed an unbeaten season with a 20-14 victory over Ohio State. It was the springboard win to a national championship which Michigan wrapped up by beating Washington State in the Rose Bowl. But nothing can match the postgame after Ohio State for Lloyd Carr.

"I've been at Michigan since 1980, and there are tremendous highs and lows," Carr said. "I mean, I was there when Kordell Stewart threw that pass in the Colorado game. But one of the most unbelievable moments in my coaching experience was after that Ohio State game in 1997. It was one of those things that was never planned.

"We had beaten Ohio State. We were unbeaten. We were going to the Rose Bowl," Carr remembered. "So we get back into the locker room, and they present the Big Ten trophy. Then somebody came in to the locker room after all of that and said, 'Hey, the crowd is still out there, and we're going back out!'

"To go back out there, into that Stadium," Lloyd said with pride, "I mean it gives me goose bumps every time I think about it. To go back out is something that had never happened, at least not to my knowledge, ever before. For that to be the last moment in that Stadium for those kids, the seniors, was the most special moment in that Stadium I've ever had."

Certainly, that moment stands out for Carr, but he's got plenty of others. Lloyd is a guy with a great sense of perspective. And while the postgame after Ohio State was special, he also told me about the great sense of responsibility he feels as the leader of the program. This sense comes from his years of watching and learning from those who came before him.

"My first seven years at Michigan," Lloyd said, "I was in the press box for games. The next three years, I was on the sidelines with Bo. Just to be by his side was special. It's an experience I appreciate more as time goes by.

"It never failed to be exciting to walk down that tunnel, and run on that field," Lloyd mused. "It's like when you're playing or coaching, you never think it's going to end. What you would like to do, is that every single time you walk down that tunnel or run on that field, you should appreciate it. You should realize how lucky you are, and know that it's not going to last."

I get the feeling that Lloyd Carr has thought about it. He's realized how fortunate he is. As a former football letter-winner and alum, I'm glad Lloyd Carr is the man in charge. His sense of tradition, and what it means to be a part of Michigan football, will be passed along to hundreds of young men as long as he coaches. Thanks, Coach. We are lucky indeed.

Lloyd Carr: Appreciate it, every time.

"I Had Just Coached My Last Game
in Michigan Stadium"

Bo Schembechler has never been the type to spring surprises. So it was a pretty major surprise when Bo announced at the end of the 1989 season that he would retire as Michigan's coach after the Rose Bowl game on New Year's Day 1990. It was a surprise because Bo had just completed two of his most successful seasons. He had led Michigan to a pair of Big Ten championships in 1988 and 1989. The Wolverines had gone through those two years without a conference loss. The closest they came to losing was a tie at Illinois in 1988. Despite two heart bypass surgeries during his career at Michigan, Bo looked healthy and was coaching his best.

Bo knew it was over long before any of us did, though. After beating Ohio State 28-18 in 1989, he was interviewed on the field by ABC television. "Somebody said when ABC field reporter Mike Adamle interviewed me after that game," Bo recalls, "that I didn't even smile. Probably the reason for that was I realized then, that I had just coached my last game in Michigan Stadium."

It wasn't until a couple of weeks later that Bo let everybody know at a press conference that he was through. "I'm sad at leaving," Bo told the gathered press. "I hate to leave the players. I hate to leave coaching, but it's time to go."

Just like he was during his career, Bo was direct and to the point. It was a no-nonsense announcement. In retrospect, Bo knew it was the right thing to do for himself and his family. But as you might expect, he didn't go without a fight. "Since the second heart operation, my doctors had been after me to slow down," Bo laughs. "They kept telling me I just couldn't keep going like this. I was 60 years old, and they told me I couldn't keep pushing myself. The doctors told me they didn't feel that I could ever just step back to a lesser role because I was too conscientious. They told me the only way I could do it was to divorce myself from the athletic program.

"With all that weighing on me, I knew I had to go," Bo says matter-of-factly. "And when I made the decision to retire, I never

Bo heads into retirement.

looked back, and I still don't. It was the right thing to do. It was the right time to do it," Bo says with great pride. "It was the job I loved the most. I'll never have a job like the one I left. It was the most gratifying job that I'll ever have. But I walked away and the program was intact. It was not in disarray. I was not chased out of town. There were no violations of recruiting rules that forced me to resign. And all of the great people that contributed over my 21 years were still with me, and that is unheard of in intercollegiate athletics. To be able to do that made me very, very proud."

Schembechler may have stopped coaching Michigan, but he never left Michigan football. The issue was not that he didn't want to coach anymore; rather, it was that he couldn't coach the only way he knew how. "In my prime, I could coach any position, anywhere, anyhow," Bo says with conviction. "I could study film for eight hours a day and never stop. I could do all those things, but it was coming to the point where maybe I couldn't do it anymore. I didn't want to go on and on and on, to where the job became a burden. I didn't want it to become too hard for me to do. If I couldn't be the guy that I was before, and I couldn't coach all-out, then let's get somebody else in here that could."

Bo has never been the kind of person to hype himself. He has never said that he's anything more than a football coach. He staunchly defends his former occupation as an honorable profession. He is modest and spreads the credit around. Even as he stepped down as coach, he deflected the credit. "It could have been somebody else that got the Michigan job in 1969," Bo says, "and probably done the same things that I've done, maybe even better."

There are many who would argue with Bo about that, including yours truly. He is a remarkable man, and his accomplishments at Michigan are legendary. Hundreds of young men are better off today than when they enrolled at Michigan because of their association with Bo. There is one thing he unashamedly admits that he did bring with him when he accepted the job at Michigan that Bo feels nobody else would have, "If anybody else would have taken this job, there is one thing I know for sure. They wouldn't have had the respect for the job like I had. It was the best thing that ever happened to me in my life."

You Can Feel the Tradition

There are a great many traditions that surround Michigan Stadium. As players, you get to tap the "Go Blue Go" plaque that hangs above the door of the locker room before you head out to play a game. Jumping up and touching the "M" Club banner as you run across the field to start a game is thrilling. For fans, the tradition of tailgate parties and specific menus for specific games draw folks back to Michigan Stadium in record numbers every fall.

One of the newest traditions for the players was started by Lloyd Carr, the Michigan head coach since 1995. It is a tradition of which I was unaware until I started to write this book. While talking to Scott Dreisbach, a former Michigan quarterback, I found out about it.

Scott and I were discussing his great finish against Virginia in 1995 when he brought the Wolverines back from a 17-0 deficit in the final 12 minutes to rescue an 18-17 win. His touchdown pass to Mercury Hayes as time expired is one of the great finishes in Michigan Stadium history. But Dreisbach said he missed one of the great traditions of Michigan football immediately after the game. "The reporters rushed me after the game," Dreisbach recalled, "and wanted to talk to me. It was my first game, and I didn't know any better, so I talked to them on the field about the finish. Well, I missed the team singing 'The Victors' in the locker room after the game."

Dreisbach said he got in a little trouble for his absence. "Coach Carr told me we don't do interviews on the field. We come into the locker room as a team and sing 'The Victors' after a win. I had never been asked to be interviewed before, so I didn't know," Dreisbach laughed, "but I never missed after that."

Scott says he was disappointed he missed that traditional moment in his first game, but then he asked me if I knew about visiting the Stadium at night. I told him I wasn't aware of a team function like that. He then started to tell me about the new tradition that Coach Carr had started when he took over as coach.

"Right before we ended our early fall practices," Scott began, "Coach Carr would take us all over to the Stadium late at night. It was maybe nine o'clock or so, and he would have the whole team walk from the football building to the Stadium. We'd walk down the tunnel, and everybody would be quiet. There were no lights on. You could just hear the crowd. You could just feel the tradition late at night all alone in the Stadium under the stars." Dreisbach sighed and concluded, "It's a great place to play."

After hearing this story, I had to talk with Coach Carr about this new tradition. Surprisingly, the idea for this quiet, reflective exercise for the team came from a legendary broadcaster. "I had read an article during the summer," Lloyd remembered, "and the great ABC college football announcer, Keith Jackson, was the subject of the article. Jackson talked about college football, and what he loved about college football. The thing he said he loved most about college football was the tradition. In the course of the article, Jackson was quoted as saying that if you really want to know what tradition is, some Friday evening at about nine o'clock, you should go into Michigan Stadium and look around."

Carr continued by saying that Jackson explained it very clearly. "Jackson said that you can feel the spirit. You can feel the ghosts of all the great games, and all the great players, and all the great coaches, who have built the tradition at Michigan."

Carr says he was riveted by Jackson's remarks, and they made a huge impression on him. "Honestly," Lloyd said, "I thought it was an incredible statement, and it really summed up what Michigan is all about."

Carr told me he decided to do it. "The kids probably thought I was crazy," Lloyd laughed. "The Friday night before camp ended, a week before the first game, we had meetings at Schembechler Hall. When we broke from our meetings at about nine o'clock, I said, 'OK, men, follow me.' So we walked across the practice fields, and over the railroad tracks to the Stadium."

When they got down the tunnel and on to the field, Carr said he addressed the team. "I told them there was a changing of the guard here. There was a new group of seniors leading the team in their last year, and there was a new group of freshmen coming in starting their own tradition.

"I told them this team has a short lifespan," Lloyd continued, "and it's what you do with it that's going to decide what kind of legacy you leave here. We then broke up, and the position coaches took their players around the Stadium. They talked to them about some of the games they remembered, and some of the plays they remembered. Then every guy spent some time alone.

"It's been something that I've done every year since then," Carr said. "And that trip to the Stadium has become a part of our tradition. It's amazing, because from a player's freshman year to his senior year, there is a great change. When those seniors go in for the last time, they have a lot of memories. It really helps them understand the importance of their senior year."

I told Coach Carr someday I'd like to take that trip. I'm 30 years removed from my playing days, but I can guarantee I'd be emotionally moved. I can't think of a better way to spend an autumn evening in Ann Arbor than sitting under the stars, alone in Michigan Stadium with the ghosts and tradition of Michigan football. I'll say hello to Yost, Crisler, and Ufer for you.

A Closing Note

It has been a real treat for me to write this collection of stories. I've learned a lot about Michigan Stadium that I didn't know before. To be frank, the process has given me a greater appreciation for the Stadium. I didn't think that was possible, but after talking with so many people who have been moved by their experiences at the corner of Stadium and Main, I must say that the word *shrine* comes to mind.

True, it is just a stadium. It is just a place where people gather to watch a sporting event. But it is also the home for countless un-forgettable memories of players, coaches, and fans alike. From its opening in 1927 to the present day, it has changed very little. From the very beginning it has been a foundation of the Michigan football tradition. Somehow, that makes it more than just a place.

So many other great venues have been razed or abandoned in the name of progress. Michigan Stadium still stands tall as a monument to the people who built the unmatched tradition of Michigan football.

The next time you are there, think about Yost, jumping back and forth over the goal-line. Think about Harmon effortlessly gliding in for a score. Think about Crisler standing with austere command on the sidelines. Think about Oosterbaan and his ashes scattered over the hallowed ground on the field. Think about Canham nervously pacing behind the press box. Think about Schembechler barking plays into his quarterback's ear. Think about Carter dancing down the sideline with a pass. Think about Ufer, with his arms upraised in the press box squeezing the scoring horn. Think about Woody Hayes kicking a down marker. Think about Leach pitching the ball on an option at the last moment. Think about Howard diving for a ball that can't be caught. Think about the band roaring out of the tunnel playing "The Victors."

You get the idea. Think about your favorite moment. There are thousands of them, and they all live on in Michigan Stadium.

Celebrate the Variety of Michigan and American Sports in These Other New Releases from Sports Publishing!

Michigan: Where Have You Gone?
by Jim Cnockaert

- 6 x 9 hardcover
- 250 pages
- photos throughout
- $19.95 (2004 release)

Riding with the Blue Moth
by Bill Hancock

- 6 x 9 hardcover
- 256 pages
- photos throughout
- $24.95

Tales from Michigan Stadium: Volume II
by Jim Brandstatter

- 5.5 x 8.25 hardcover
- 200 pages
- photos throughout
- $19.95 (2005 release)

Mike Ditka: Reflections on the 1985 Bears
by Mike Ditka with Rick Telander

- 5.5 x 8.25 hardcover
- 200 pages
- photos throughout
- $19.95

Charlie Sanders's Tales from the Detroit Lions
by Charlie Sanders with Larry Paladino

- 5.5 x 8.25 hardcover
- 192 pages
- photos throughout
- $19.95

The Holyfield Way: What I Learned from Evander
by Jim Thomas with commentary by Evander Holyfield

- 6 x 9 hardcover • 256 pages
- eight-page photo insert
- $24.95

Detroit Pistons: Champions at Work
by The Detroit News

- 8.5 x 11 hard/softcover
- 128 pages • color photos
- $19.95 (hardcover)
- $14.95 (trade paper)

Dick Enberg: Oh My!
by Dick Enberg with Jim Perry

- 6 x 9 hardcover • 256 pages
- 16-page color-photo section
- $24.95
- Bonus "Beyond the Book" DVD included!

Tales of the Magical Spartans
by Tim Staudt and Fred Stabley Jr.

- 5.5 x 8.25 hardcover
- 200 pages
- photos throughout
- $19.95 (2003 release)

Ferdie Pacheco: Blood in My Coffee
by Ferdie Pacheco

- 6 x 9 hardcover
- 256 pages
- photo insert
- $24.95